About th

Joe Castello was born in 1939. He graduated in Pharmacy and then created a small chain of pharmacies. He is now retired.

He was active in rugby, judo and skiing until common sense prevailed. He still plays in a 9-piece jazz and blues band.

The large spacings in the text have been introduced to help readers who have the disadvantage of dyslexia.

Joe Castello

THE JOE PUBLIC GUIDE TO THE ROMAN CATHOLIC CHURCH

AUSTIN MACAULEY PUBLISHERS™

LONDON · CAMBRIDGE · NEW YORK · SHARJAH

A CIP catalogue record for this title is available from the British Library.

ISBN 9781398431508 (Paperback)
ISBN 9781398431515 (ePub e-book)

www.austinmacauley.com

First Published 2022
Austin Macauley Publishers Ltd®
1 Canada Square
Canary Wharf
London
E14 5AA

Acknowledgements

Many thanks to Guy Willett of www.mycomputerguy.com who has not only donated the Joe Public Guide website but continues to maintain it. This ongoing generous commitment is massively appreciated.

Thanks also to James Wells of www.wells-design.co.uk for generously donating the graphics for the front cover. This is the third cover that James has created for me.

My thanks to Father David Donaghue and to John Day for giving incredibly constructive feedback on those chapters that I consulted them about.

Table of Contents

Introduction

The Roman Catholic Church is the original church of Christianity.

Because it's the oldest, it's the Church from which all other Christian denominations are derived.

The Roman Catholic Church has over 1.2 billion adherents.

Along with these facts, it is also the most structured and by far the wealthiest church.

This book was written in 2019 by a non-Catholic for the benefit of other non-Catholics who have a natural curiosity regarding powerful and long-lasting institutions which have been very influential over so many people's lives.

Along with other books in The Joe Public Guide series, it reduces a complex subject down to a summary of headlines which make for easy reading. Its purpose is to give an overview. There are of course thousands of books that can give greater knowledge to those whose appetite is merely whetted by this publication.

Sources of information include:

- The news magazine THE WEEK.
- INTRODUCING CHRISTIANITY, by Anthony O'Hear and Judy Groves.
- THE GUIDE TO THE ROMAN CATHOLIC CHURCH, by Edmund Hartley.
- WIKIPEDIA.
- THE CASE OF THE POPE, by Geoffrey Robertson QC.
- IN GOD'S NAME, by David Yallop.
- COSA NOSTRA, by John Dickie.
- CATHOLICISM FOR DUMMIES by Rev. John Trigilio PhD, ThD and Rev. Kenneth Brighenti PhD.
- THE VATICAN EXPOSED by Paul L Williams.

1. The Life of Jesus Christ

Jesus Christ, also known as Jesus of Nazareth, was born over 2,000 years ago.

It is therefore totally understandable that some of the information about him may be rather vague and sometimes contradictory.

He was born in Palestine which at that time, was part of the Roman Empire.

His home town was Nazareth in Galilee which is north of Judea.

He died around 30–33 AD at age 33 in Jerusalem, which is located in Judea.

The cause of his death was crucifixion which was a particularly unpleasant form of execution that was reserved for non-Roman criminals. His death was witnessed by his mother.

His parents were Mary and Joseph and it is believed by Christians that Jesus was miraculously conceived by the Holy Spirit in Mary's womb when she was still a virgin but at a time when she was betrothed to Joseph of Nazareth.

The virgin birth is central to the Christian belief system.

When Joseph was troubled by Mary's pregnancy, he was said to have had 3 dreams, during the 1st of which, an angel assured him that Mary's baby was God's work.

The Nativity (birth) story was only referred to in the Gospels by Matthew and Luke.

Matthew's version claims that 3 wise men from the East, following a star, brought gifts to the baby Jesus and recognised him as King of the Jews.

On hearing of Jesus' birth, King Herod wanted him dead and ordered the killing of all male infants in Bethlehem who were 2 years or under. This became known as "the massacre of the innocents". But it is believed that an angel warned Joseph of this danger in his second dream, and so the family fled to Egypt – later to return and live in Nazareth.

In this version, there is no manager, no stable, no census and no shepherds.

In Luke's version of the nativity, Mary learned from the angel Gabriel that she would conceive and bear a child called Jesus through the action of the Holy Spirit. When Mary was due to give birth, she and Joseph travelled from Nazareth to Joseph's ancestral home in Bethlehem to register in the census ordered by Caesar Augustus. Whilst there, Mary gave birth to Jesus, and, as they had found no room in the inn, she placed the new-born in a manger. Legend has it that an angel announced the birth to local shepherds who left their flocks and went to Bethlehem to see the baby Jesus and that they then subsequently spread the news.

After the presentation of Jesus at the temple, Joseph, Mary and Jesus returned to Nazareth in Galilee.

In this version, there is no star, no wise men and no flight to Egypt.

Jesus was born a Jew of Jewish parents. It follows that he was circumcised when he was 8 days old.

He went on to be the elder brother of James, Joseph, Judas, Simon and his unnamed sisters.

Jesus is the central figure of Christianity, whom the teachings of all Christian denominations believe to be the Son of God. The term Christian is used to define "one who owes allegiance to the person Christ" or is simply "a follower of Christ".

Christianity regards Jesus as the awaited Messiah prophesied in the Hebrew Bible (the Old Testament) and refers to him as Jesus Christ, a name that is also used in non-Christian contexts.

Virtually all modern scholars of antiquity agree that Jesus existed historically, and historians consider that the Gospels of Matthew, Mark, Luke and John are the best sources for investigating the biography of historical Jesus.

These gospels are 4 accounts, each written by a different author. They often differ in content and in the ordering of events, although there is a greater similarity between Matthew, Mark and Luke. They were written over the following time-lines:

- The Gospel of Mark (written 60–75 AD)
- The Gospel of Matthew (written 65–85 AD)
- The Gospel of Luke (written 65–95 AD)
- The Gospel of John (written 75–100 AD)

Most scholars agree that Jesus was a Galilean Jewish rabbi who preached his message orally in the Aramaic language, was baptised by John the Baptist, and was crucified by the order of the Roman Prefect, Pontius Pilate.

It is also generally recognised that Jesus had a public ministry that lasted for no more than 3 years. Despite being so short, it was incredibly effective.

It is also agreed that John the Baptist preceded Jesus, was Jewish until his involvement with Jesus, and that their ministries overlapped.

John initially wanted Jesus to baptise him, but Jesus persuaded John to baptise Him instead. At this point, some of John's followers became disciples (followers) of Jesus.

After he was baptised, Jesus then spent 40 days fasting in the wilderness during which time it is believed that the devil came to tempt him, but without success.

The gospels indicate that Jesus could read, paraphrase, and debate scripture, but do not imply that he had formal scribal training.

He frequently used parables and miracles to teach people about the Kingdom of God. He also called on people to devote their lives to God and told his followers to adhere strictly to Jewish law.

Jesus' mission was first and foremost to the Jews, and only secondarily to the Gentiles (non-Jews).

We should remember that his 1st followers were pious Jews who must have believed in his reforming ideas and values.

It is useful to remember that Christianity began as a Jewish sect that was preached to Jews by Jews, who saw themselves as a reformed version of the Jewish faith.

All of the ethical teachings of Jesus include loving one's enemies, refraining from hatred and lust, and turning the other cheek. The approximately 30 parables that he delivers in the gospels, constitute about 30% of Jesus' recorded teachings.

Jesus' moral message includes such things as:

- Purity of heart.
- Humility.
- Loving thy neighbour.
- Un-aggressiveness.
- The lack of importance of wealth.
- The corrupting effect of wealth and success.
- Doing unto others as you would have done unto yourself.

There are however many contradictory and controversial sayings in the gospels.

According to the gospels, Jesus devotes a large portion of his ministry to performing miracles, especially healings. The miracles can be classified into 2 main categories: healing miracles and nature miracles. The healing miracles included cures for physical ailments, exorcisms, and resurrections of the dead. The nature miracles showed Jesus' power over nature and included turning water into wine, walking on water, and the calming of the storm. All of the miracles teach the importance of faith.

There were 2 distinct geographical settings for Jesus' ministry. The 1st took place north of Judea, in Galilee, where he conducted a successful ministry and chose his 12 apostles whose identities vary in the different gospels. You could describe the apostles as primary disciples who were sent forth to preach Jesus's message.

In addition to these, there was a much larger group of close followers who were keen to learn more about the new ministry and who were referred to as his disciples.

The 2nd and final ministry showed that Jesus was rejected and killed when he travelled to Jerusalem in Judea.

He made a grand and triumphant entry into the city on what became Palm Sunday, and during that week, he is said to have driven the money changers from the Temple. It was at this time that Judas Iscariot, one of the 12 apostles, bargained to betray him for 30 silver coins.

This period culminated in the Last Supper that Jesus shared with the 12 apostles.

This supper was a ritual Jewish Passover meal that became known as the Last Supper, and it must be remembered that Passover is a very sensitive time when Jews celebrate their exodus from Egypt. During the meal, Jesus predicted that one of his apostles would betray him.

After the Last Supper, Jesus visited the garden of Gethsemane and it was here that he was duly betrayed by Judas and arrested at the behest of the Jewish priests and elders. His teachings were clearly offensive to most orthodox Jews of the time. The 4 gospels have slightly different accounts of this incident.

After the arrest, Jesus was taken to Pontius Pilate's Court but the Roman Governor proved to be extremely reluctant to condemn Jesus. The Jewish elders desperately wanted him to be found guilty of claiming to be the King of the Jews. Pilate realised that Jesus was a Galilean, and thus came under the jurisdiction of Herod Antipas. Jesus was sent to Herod but was duly returned without trial. At this point, Pilate called together the Jewish elders and announced that he was unable to find Jesus guilty.

Observing a Passover custom of the time, Pilate allowed 1 prisoner, chosen by the crowd, to be released. He gave the people a choice between Jesus and a murderer called Barabbas. He had anticipated that Jesus would be chosen. Persuaded by the Jewish elders, however, the mob chose to release Barabbas and to crucify Jesus.

Pilate then wrote a sign in Hebrew, Latin and Greek that read "Jesus of Nazareth, the King of the Jews" (abbreviated to INRI in depictions), to be affixed to Jesus' cross.

He was scourged and taunted as he was made to carry the cross along Via Dolorosa to Mount Calvary to be crucified. At Calvary, Jesus was offered a concoction which served as a painkiller. According to the gospels, he refused it. The soldiers then placed a Crown of Thorns on Jesus's head and proceeded to ridicule him as he was crucified between 2 convicted thieves. The Roman soldiers broke the legs of the 2 thieves', which was a procedure designed to hasten death, but they didn't break those of Jesus because he was already dead. They then cast lots for his clothes.

On the same day, Joseph of Arimathea, with Pilate's permission, removed Jesus' body from the cross and wrapped it in a clean cloth before placing it in a new rock-hewn tomb. The tomb was then secured by a large stone being rolled across the entrance. All this took place on what is now referred to as Good Friday.

All 4 gospels agree that on a Sunday morning, Mary Magdalene went to the tomb and was surprised to find it empty. Jesus had risen from the dead and then subsequently made a series of appearances to the disciples. The 4 gospels have slightly different versions of Jesus' resurrection from the dead and his ascension into Heaven. It is generally accepted however that on the 3rd day, Jesus arose from the dead and went to heaven, on what is now referred to as Easter Sunday.
Christians believe that Jesus is their role model and that he died by crucifixion as a sacrifice to achieve atonement. He then rose from the dead and ascended into heaven, from whence he will return.

The timeframe between the arrest of Jesus in the Garden of Gethsemane and his crucifixion on Mount Calvary is unclear.

Not everything in the New Testament gospels is considered to be historically reliable. Elements, where historical authenticity is disputed include the Nativity, the Resurrection, the Ascension and some of Jesus' miracles. Non-Christians and secular people clearly find it difficult to believe in the fundamental principle of miracles which is a foundation stone of Christianity.

After Jesus' death on Friday, and after they found his tomb empty on Sunday, the risen Jesus appeared before his disciples who became convinced that he was alive. The community that they formed separated from Judaism and became the early Christian church, which was the precursor of the Roman Catholic Church.

Contemporary scholarship places Jesus firmly in the Jewish tradition and sees him as the founder of a renewal movement within Judaism. To some, he is seen as an egalitarian prophet of social change.

The last week of Jesus' life in Jerusalem and the sequence of events leading up to his crucifixion, is known as the Passion.
The great majority of Christians (but not all) worship Jesus as the incarnation of God the Son, the second of 3 persons of a Divine or Holy Trinity – God the Father, God the Son (Jesus) and God the Holy Ghost.

Matthew traces Jesus' ancestry to Abraham through David, whilst Luke traces it to God through Adam.

Christianity in general and the Catholic Church in particular, are very committed to the use of depictions of Jesus. These take the form of religious paintings, effigies and icons. These show Jesus as a baby in the nativity setting, as a child and as an adult. Adult imagery includes his presence with His disciples, the apostles, the sick and his general followers. There are obviously huge numbers of variations on the theme of the crucifixion. The purpose of these artefacts is to remind and focus attention on the core values of the Christian faith. Most Catholic churches are filled with these icons, which marks the greatest possible contrast to Islamic mosques, where all imagery of the Prophet Muhammad is banned. This is well illustrated in the mosques of Spain's Seville and Cordoba.

There is no scholarly consensus which endorses the authenticity of any relic attributed to Jesus. The false claims of pieces of wood from the cross used in the crucifixion would be enough to construct many fine buildings!

The widely accepted calendar era, abbreviated as BC (before Christ) and AD (Anno Domini / in the year of our Lord), is based on the birth date of Jesus.

Jesus' death was seen as a way to free Jews from their obligation to submit any longer to the detail of Jewish law, such as the matrilineal line.

Once established, Christianity could and did then develop as a world religion, spreading throughout the Roman Empire and beyond, unshackled by its racial and legalistic origins. It is as a result of these continuing constraints that there are still only about 13 million Jews worldwide.

It is interesting that Christianity, and therefore the early Catholic Church emerged from a backward and rural Judean Jewish culture, to become so universal as to both engulf and outlive the Roman Empire itself.

In Islam, Jesus is considered as one of God's important prophets and the Messiah. The Qur'an mentions Jesus by name 25 times and emphasises that he was a mortal human like all other prophets, and had been divinely chosen to spread God's message.

To them, Jesus was the bringer of scripture and was miraculously born of a virgin, but he was neither the son of God nor the victim of crucifixion. According to the Qur'an, Jesus was not crucified but was physically raised into Heaven by God. His miracles were God's miracles, and he was seen as a precursor to Muhammad. Most Muslims believe that Jesus will return to earth at the end of time.

Judaism rejects both the Christian and Islamic belief that Jesus was the awaited Messiah.

In the 19th Century, approximately 60,000 "Lives of Jesus" were published in book form.

The Franco Zeffirelli film "Jesus of Nazareth" helps anyone to gain an overview of the traditional story of the life of Jesus. This film was critically acclaimed and was directed by Zeffirelli who was himself a devoted Catholic.

2. The Holy Bible

Catholics believe that God is the principal author of the Sacred Scripture (The Holy Bible) although He made use of specific people – sacred authors, who wrote in a human language, and did so at a particular time and place in history.

The Bible is a collection of <u>73 books</u> which were written by many different authors over a long period of time. It is divided into two main sections – the Old Testament which has 46 books and the New Testament which has 27 books.

The Old Testament contains the Jewish Scriptures which were written in Hebrew and were used by faithful Jews before the time of Christ. It is also known as the Hebrew Bible. In fact, the Jewish holy book, the Torah, is the 1st five books of the Old Testament.

The 10 Commandments (the Decalogue) were listed in the second Old Testament book of Exodus and were given to the frightened Hebrew people in order to keep them from sinning. It can be seen that most of the Commandments are negative instructions. Thou shall not…

Catholics believe that there can be no denial that the Hebrew scriptures constitute the historical word of God, dating as they do, initially, from around 1000 BC.

The New Testament consists of books and letters written by the early Christians. These people used the language of their time, notably Greek, Hebrew and Aramaic. They used vocabulary and wrote in a style that reflected their own personalities and education.

It is common knowledge amongst Catholics that the New Testament somehow completes the Old Testament. They believe that Christianity had been in the process of developing since the beginning of Hebrew recorded history. They therefore, see Christianity as an updated version of Judaism.

The transition from Old Testament thinking with its emphasis on Jewish traditions and law, to New Testament life, with its Christian overtones, took some time. This was probably because most of the early Christians were Jewish converts.

It is believed that God revealed his divine truths via historical acts, using events and people of his choosing. He conveyed things to people through words and actions that made use of the ways of speaking and thinking that were common at the time. It was believed that God worked in this way so that it would be possible for humans to write down or pass on these eternal truths.

The people who experienced these events and received God's divine messages either wrote them down later or would pass them on in a reliable oral tradition that was later written down under the inspiration of the Holy Spirit.

The Second Vatican Council (Vatican II) of 1962–65, states: "Everything asserted by the inspired authors or sacred writers must be held to be asserted by the Holy Spirit".

To Christians, the Holy Bible is unmatched in importance for learning about God, his plans for us, and how he has worked throughout human history for our salvation.

It is believed that God chose to reveal to us certain truths for the sake of our salvation. This message of salvation is the set of revealed truths which are called the "deposit of faith", or Divine Revelation. The Bible is primarily concerned with telling us these truths, which are without error because they are the word of God himself.

The whole point of reading and understanding the Bible is to encounter God, understand the revelation he has given us, and to grow in faith.

Scripture is a living thing, meant for all people in all times and all places.

Catholics believe that God speaks through it now, just as much as he did when it was written.

The initial versions of the Bible were later translated into Latin, before eventually being translated to a whole host of local languages.

For example, in Britain, we have the King James version which was written in the early 1600s AD. It follows that the Poles and the Spaniards have their own language versions.

With estimated total world sales of over 5 billion copies, the Bible is widely considered to be the best-selling book of all time.

It currently enjoys annual sales of over 100 million copies and has been a major influence on literature and history, especially in the West where it was the 1st mass-printed book. The Gutenberg bible was the 1st bible to be printed using movable type.

Readers will note that the evolution of the Bible is very different from that of the Muslim holy book – The Koran.

The Koran was created during the lifetime of the Prophet Muhammad and was recited by him to a vast following just before he died in 632 AD at the age of 62.
Soon after this, 6 authentic versions were copied, and then all other versions were destroyed. These authentic versions were all in Arabic, and it remains the position that the only valid versions of the Koran are in Arabic.

Muslims claim that by not accepting translations of their Holy Book, both unintentional and mischievous interpretations have been avoided.

3. The History of the Catholic Church

The Christian religion is based on the teachings of Jesus Christ, who lived and preached in the 1st century in the provinces of Galilee and Judea in the Roman Empire.

Christianity and therefore Roman Catholicism are the development of Judaism which is the oldest monotheistic religion in the world. All Christian rules were inherited from Jewish traditions.

Catholic doctrine teaches that the contemporary Catholic Church is the continuation of this early Christian community that was established by Jesus.

After the death of Christ, tradition says that Peter the Apostle, who Christ had appointed as leader, went to Rome where he was regarded as the 1st Bishop of Rome and therefore as the 1st Pope. He held this position from about 48 AD until he was eventually betrayed and put to death in about 68 AD.
He was crucified in the upside-down position, by his own request, because he didn't feel worthy of the same death as Jesus.

Christianity spread throughout the Roman Empire, despite early persecutions by the pagan state. Refusal to "Emperor worship" was seriously punishable and Paul was consequently beheaded by Nero (as opposed to crucified, because he was a Roman citizen).

When the Jewish temple in Jerusalem was destroyed in around 70 AD, the diaspora of the new Christianity was accelerated and the centre of Christianity moved from Jerusalem to Rome. As previously mentioned, most, if not all of the early Christians were converts from Judaism.

Emperor Constantine legalised Christianity in 313 AD before he moved the imperial capital to Constantinople (now Istanbul in Turkey). Constantine then later adopted the Catholic Church as his own religion, even though it was both poor and persecuted. In order to be fit for purpose for the mighty Roman Empire, the Catholic Church needed upgrading and re-branding.

This was achieved by Constantine transferring vast wealth to the Vatican and then encouraging it to immerse itself in overt and extreme pomp and circumstance.

The Pope was given great status and became both incredibly wealthy and incredibly powerful – all of which was a total contrast to the previous 300 years.

Constantine then called a meeting of all the bishops within the Church. It was held in Nicaea in 325 AD and from it came the Nicene Creed which affirmed the Faith.

The creed was updated in 381 AD in Constantinople. This revision produced the creed which became the state religion within the Roman Empire and with which modern Christians are familiar.

In 330, during the reign of Constantine, the Roman Empire had become split into 2. Rome became the centre of the western part, whilst Constantinople became the centre of the eastern part and was called Byzantium. During this period Rome took on huge importance for Christians.

A little later, in the 6th and 7th centuries, the advent of Islam and the expansion of the Muslim empire caused a severing of the connection and relationship between Rome and Byzantium.

Later Germanic invaders of Roman territory eventually adopted Catholicism in order to ally themselves with the papacy and the monasteries.

The Middle Ages (around 500 AD – 1500 AD) saw the Christian harassment of Jews and Muslims. Those found guilty of heresy were brutally treated.

By the end of the 6th Century, when there was no longer an emperor of Rome, the Bishop of Rome therefore, became recognised not only as the head of The Church in the West but also as a person of great political power.

This in turn led to the East-West schism of the 11th century (1054) which split the Church into the Catholic and Orthodox Churches. Some of the latter retained a connection with Rome and formed what is called the Eastern Catholic Churches.

From 1096–1487, The Catholic Church was centrally involved in all the Crusades against Islam, with the aim of restoring the Holy Land of Palestine to Christian control.

1478 saw the beginning of the Spanish Inquisition. This was a tribunal that was started in Spain. People found guilty of heresy were burnt in front of crowds in the street.

At that time, Jews and Muslims in Spain were made to convert to Catholicism and the purpose of the tribunal was to find the heretics amongst the converts. It was the strategy used to uphold the religious orthodoxy of the Catholic Church.

We need to remember that the Muslims from North Africa (the Moors) had previously dominated Spain for almost 800 years.

The tribunal wasn't formally disbanded until 1834 and it was estimated that 3,000–5,000 people had been executed during its existence.

The Roman Catholic Church became the dominant influence in Western civilisation right up to the modern age.

Despite this, the 1500s saw a challenge by the Protestant Reformation which was instigated by Martin Luther in Germany. John Calvin was another prominent challenger.

Martin Luther was a German Roman Catholic Augustine monk from the small town of Wittenberg which was part of the Holy Roman Empire.

He rose to fame in 1521, when he challenged the corruption of the Roman Catholic Church.

He denounced the Catholic Church's sale of "indulgences". These were a cash-cow for the Church and represented cash for forgiveness.

Luther thought that this was disgusting behaviour for a Church that was already incredibly wealthy and which already owned about 50% of the land in Europe.

At the time, he thought that his actions would help to reform the Church, rather than divide it. He saw himself as a reformer, not as a saboteur.

He rejected the Pope and the Church as the ultimate authority and claimed that it was the bible that had the ultimate authority.

He was convinced that the righteous person lives by faith alone.

As part of his ideas for reform, he also advocated that church services should be held in local languages and that they should contain many more hymns.

It's true that Luther's reforms gave birth to the Protestant movement and as a result he was condemned as a heretic by the Roman Catholic Church.

Luther was a man of tremendous principle who found it impossible to make a religious compromise, but totally rejected the idea of force being used to reach his objectives.

His writings included some very anti-Semitic beliefs, which may well have been prompted by the death of Christ.

In any event, these writings were quoted by Hitler in his persecution of the Jews centuries later, in the 1930s.

Interestingly, many years later, a black American civil rights activist was so impressed by Luther's principled effectiveness, combined with his total rejection of violence, that he changed his name.

Michael King renamed himself as Martin Luther King senior, and his son as Martin Luther King junior.

The break away from the Catholic Church by Henry V111 of England in the 1530s was solely a political matter because the Pope was unable to grant Henry a divorce from his 1st wife (Catherine of Aragon) so that he could marry his mistress. This was because Catherine's nephew had his army occupying Rome at the time. The Pope didn't wish to cause offence!

In England during Tudor times, the Catholics were persecuted by the Protestants, beginning with the dissolution of the monasteries. In other words, these Catholic possessions were stolen by Henry V111.

Later, during the reign of Henry's Catholic daughter Mary 1st, the fires of Smithfield marked the persecution of the Protestants by Catholics. This persecution was short-lived and the pendulum swung again when the protestant Queen Elizabeth 1st came to the throne.

The 1600s then saw a challenge by secular individuals in the Enlightenment.

Also, during the 1600s and 1700s, there was the forcible removal of about 90% of the land in Ireland from its Catholic landlords. This was repeated in the 1800s in

Germany when the Catholic Church lands were secularised.

The 18th century however saw the rise of Napoleon and the re-establishment of the dominance of the Catholic Church and the re-establishment of the Papal States.

Due to donations from the faithful, The Catholic Church had become very rich and many within The Church departed greatly from the simple lifestyle of Jesus. Bishoprics were worth having and Church zealots militantly pursued missionary aims far afield. As a result, Spanish and Portuguese explorers together with their missionaries spread the Catholic influence through Africa, Asia and the New World.

In 1870, the First Vatican Council declared the dogma of papal infallibility. The Pope had a few years earlier proclaimed the "immaculate conception" as dogma. A dogma is a definitive article of faith.

From 750 till 1860, all the Papal States were governed by the Pope and by the Vatican. They were collectively referred to as the Holy See. During that period the Holy See possessed large territories, fought wars, and entered into diplomatic alliances, all under the sovereign rule of the Pope. These territorial possessions created considerable taxes and vast wealth for the Vatican. It was therefore devastating to its finances when in 1860, the Vatican was dispossessed of its Italian papal states as a result of the creation of the new Garibaldi inspired nation of Italy. The final nail in the financial coffin was in 1870 when the Kingdom of Italy finally annexed the city of Rome, which was the last of the Papal States. In the meantime, much of northern Europe had rejected the Catholic faith in favour of Protestantism, which meant that they too were not paying taxes and tribute to the Vatican. As a result, the Vatican's wealth soon disappeared and its finances were in a desperate and catastrophic state. The state of the Vatican buildings deteriorated into appalling conditions. The Catholic Church was skint.

In 1929, during the political dominance of Italy's Benito Mussolini, the 108.7 acres of land on which the Vatican is located, was restored as an independent sovereign state by the Lateran Treaties. In these treaties, the Holy See acknowledged Italian sovereignty over the former Papal States and Italy recognised papal sovereignty over Vatican City as a new sovereign and independent state. Mussolini also lavished large financial donations on the Vatican as part of his overall strategy. Suddenly the Vatican's financial plight was reversed and the accumulation of wealth could begin again.

Since the Holy See was again a state, the Pope thereby acquired "head of state" immunity. This means that he can never be sued, nor prosecuted. It also means that the Holy See has state immunity, which with certain exceptions removes its liability for civil wrongs.

Statehood is attributed to the Holy See on the strength of its ownership of a block of land in Rome. It gives the Catholic Church all sorts of advantages that are denied to other religions. Most significantly is the Holy See's status at the UN as a "non-member state" (the only other one is Palestine). This means that it can do pretty much all that a full state member can do, except vote. And its army of diplomats is able to use this privileged status by actively promoting its uncompromising views on divorce, homosexuality, birth control, abortion and IVF.

The Pope is the supreme commander – the absolute ruler of the Vatican and head of the Holy See, which has its own "secretary of state". There are also a set of ministers and institutes that deal with subjects ranging from political questions and diplomacy to liturgy and the appointment of bishops.

The Holy See conducts diplomatic relations of some kind with 178 counties, although only about a third of this number actually sends ambassadors to Rome.

The Holy See maintains a network of diplomatic posts and dispatches ambassadors to countries with significant Catholic populations.

The Pope is regarded as the last absolute monarch serving until death, at which time the Curia meets in the Sistine Chapel to elect his successor. This result is signalled by puffs of white smoke and the cry "Habemus papam!" – we have a pope.

On its official website, the Vatican describes itself as an "absolute monarchy" in which the "Head of State is the Pope, who holds full legislative, executive and judicial powers".

He delegates the daily running of the Vatican to a Pontifical Commission of Cardinals which he personally appoints.

Following the atheistic Bolshevik Russian Revolution in 1917, all religions including the Catholic Church were brutally persecuted in the newly created Soviet Union.

In the 1936–39 Spanish Civil War, the Catholic hierarchy allied itself to Franco's Nationalists and the

Monarchy, against the Popular Front government, citing Republican violence against the Church.

The war was brutal and atrocities were committed by both sides before Franco was eventually the victor. His harsh dictatorship scarred the nation for many years.

During World War 2 (1939–45) the Catholic Church publicly condemned the Nazi movement and its aggressive acts.

Whilst Pope Pius X11 has been credited with helping to save hundreds of thousands of Jews during the Holocaust, the Church has also been accused of encouraging centuries of anti-Semitism and not doing enough to stop the Nazi atrocities.

Considerable problems continued after 1945 when freedom of religion was restricted in those countries that were aligned with the Soviet Union but had large Catholic populations. This problem was later resolved in the 1990s by the break-up of the Soviet Union into its 15 component parts.

The 1949 Chinese Civil War and the Cultural Revolution of the 1960s also caused devastating problems for Catholics and the Catholic Church in China.

In the 1960s, the Second Vatican Council led to several controversial reforms that were designed to make the Catholic Church more user-friendly. These reforms were initiated by Pope John XX111 and were harshly criticised by the conservative/traditional wing of the Church.

They modernised the Church by allowing Mass to be conducted in local languages rather than in Latin. In addition to changes in the liturgy, it also called for improved relationships with non-Christian religions, especially Judaism. There had always been tensions between Catholics and Jews because of the historical fact that Jesus was born a Jew, but died a "Christian". His death having been orchestrated by the Jews.

In the face of increased criticism from both within and without, the Catholic Church has upheld or reaffirmed at various times, controversial and uncompromising doctrinal positions, as illustrated by its opposition to:

- Homosexuality.
- Gender change.
- Female clergy.
- Married priests who are not celibate.
- Contraception (as expressed in the document Humanae vitae).
- Abortion (even in cases of rape, incest and foetal abnormality).
- Sexual activity outside marriage.
- Remarriage following divorce without an annulment.
- Same-sex marriage.
- Euthanasia.
- Suicide.

In 1978, Pope John Paul 11, formerly the archbishop of Krakow, which was at the time located in communist Poland, became the 1st non-Italian Pope in 455 years. His 27-year pontificate was one of the longest in history.

He travelled to 129 countries and used TV and radio as a means of spreading the Church's teachings. He was deeply concerned that the world was becoming too secular and considered secularism to be the main challenge for all religions.

I realise that some of the information in this book gets repeated, but this is because it's relevant to that particular chapter heading and because some people may not read all chapters. In any event, it never hurts for some points to be reaffirmed.

4. General Information

The Catholic Church, also known as the Roman Catholic Church, is the largest Christian church and has more than 1.2 billion adherents worldwide.

It is one of the oldest religious institutions in the world and has played a prominent role in the history of Western civilisation.

As repeatedly mentioned, it is headed by the Bishop of Rome, known as the Pope, who has supreme authority over the Church. He is also the head of state for the Vatican state which is also known as the Holy See.

The principal doctrines of the Church are summarised by the Nicene Creed which teaches that there is one eternal God, who exists as 3 Persons:

- God the Father
- God the Son
- God the Holy Ghost

Together, they are known as the Holy Trinity.

God became united with human nature through the conception of Christ in the womb of the Blessed Virgin Mary.

Despite being sinless whilst on earth, Jesus allowed himself to be unjustly executed by Crucifixion, as a sacrifice of himself to reconcile God with humanity.

The Greek terminology "Christ" and the Hebrew term "Messiah", both mean "anointed one".

The Roman Catholic Church is also distinguished by its celebration of the 7 sacraments which are covered in more detail in later chapters.

The Catholic Church teaches that it is the one true church that was founded by Jesus Christ, that its bishops are the successors of Christ's apostles, and that the Pope is the successor to Saint Peter who was the 1st pope.

The Church maintains that the doctrine of faith and morals that it declares as definitive, is infallible.

The Latin Church of Rome, the autonomous Eastern Catholic Churches and the religious communities such as the Jesuits, mendicant orders, and enclosed monastic orders, reflect the variety of theological options within the Church.

The Church venerates Mary as the Mother of God. Devotions to Mary are part of Catholic piety but are distinct from the worship of God.

It teaches that through divine intervention she gave birth to Jesus whilst still a virgin. The teachings include:

- Her immaculate conception without original sin.
- Her status as the Mother of God.
- Her bodily Assumption to Heaven at the end of her earthly life.

Integral to Catholicism, apart from the spreading of the Gospel are the 7 virtues, exemplified in Catholic social teaching as support for the sick, the poor and the afflicted through works of mercy. It is a fact that the Catholic Church is the largest non-governmental provider of education and medical services in the world.

Legal matters within the Church are dealt with by the application of Canon Law.

These laws are created and enforced by the Church hierarchy. They are totally separate and distinct from the common and civil law of the dioceses.

Canon law has all the ordinary elements of a mature legal system:

- Laws
- Courts
- Lawyers
- Judges
- A fully articulated legal code
- Principles of legal interpretation
- Coercive penalties that are limited to moral coercion

Currently, the 1983 Code of Canon Law is primarily used for the Latin Church of Rome.

The distinct 1990 Code of Canons for the Eastern Church, applies solely to the autonomous Eastern Catholic Churches.

The Catholic Church is made up of 24 autonomous particular churches, each of which accepts the supreme authority of the Bishop of Rome on matters of doctrine.

Their forms of worship are slightly different by virtue of their different historical and cultural influences, rather than differences in doctrine.

Each of these autonomous churches is headed by a patriarch or high-ranking bishop who exercises a degree of self-governance over particulars of its internal organisation, liturgical rites, liturgical calendar and other aspects of spirituality.

The largest by far of the particular churches is the Latin Church of Rome that reports over 1 billion followers of the 1.2 billion total adherents in the Catholic Family of churches.

Having started in Rome, it has expanded throughout Europe and then worldwide.

5. The Papacy and the Roman Curia

Peter the Apostle whose personal name was Simon, had been a fisherman and had been ordained by Jesus just before his death in about 33 AD.

As previously stated, after the death of Christ, tradition says that Peter the Apostle, who Christ had appointed leader, went to Rome where he was regarded as the 1st Bishop of Rome and therefore the 1st Pope. He held this position from about 48 AD until he was eventually betrayed and put to death in about 68 AD. He was crucified in the upside-down position, by his own request, because he didn't feel worthy of the same death as Jesus.

After Apostle Peter, it was accepted that all future Bishops of Rome (also known as Popes) were the successors to Peter and were recognised as speaking with Peter's voice.

The Pope's role as Chief Shepherd became firmly established when Emperor Constantine declared his toleration of Christianity throughout the Roman Empire in 313 AD.

The pope is the leader of the worldwide Catholic Church which is composed of the Latin Church and the Eastern

Catholic Churches which are in full communion with the Holy See of Rome.

The office of the Pope is known as the papacy.
The Catholic Church holds that Christ instituted the papacy upon giving the keys to Heaven to Saint Peter.

Directly serving the Pope is the Roman Curia, the central governing body that administers the day-to-day business of the Catholic Church, and acts like a state civil service.

It is not difficult to understand how the Pope has supreme authority in spiritual matters, but it is difficult to grasp how he also has supreme authority over the vast range of activities conducted by the Roman Curia. These activities include the management of the vast worldwide wealth that belongs to The Church and the complex financial manoeuvres associated with it. A later chapter will attempt to investigate the worldwide wealth of The Catholic Church.

The Vatican curia is a large workforce and currently employs around 2,600 people.

As mentioned in a previous chapter, the Pope is also Sovereign and the absolute monarch of Vatican City State, a small city-state entirely enclaved within the city of Rome. This is an entirely distinct entity from the Holy See.

It is from the Holy See, not as head of the Vatican City State, that the Pope receives ambassadors of states and sends them his own diplomatic representatives.

The Holy See is the total jurisdiction of the pope. It includes Vatican City and his universal ecclesiastical jurisdiction of the worldwide Catholic Church.

The position of cardinal is a high rank of honour bestowed by popes on certain clergies, such as:

- Leaders within the Roman Curia
- Bishops serving in major cities
- Distinguished theologians

Incidentally, cardinal's cassocks have 33 buttons on them, which presumably represent the number of years that Christ lived before he was crucified.

For advice and assistance in governing, the pope may turn to the College of Cardinals.

Following the death or resignation of a pope, members of the College of Cardinals who are under the age of 80, meet in a papal enclave to elect a successor. Although the enclave may theoretically elect any male Catholic as Pope, since 1389, only cardinals have been elected.

There have over the years been 265 popes. The official list has recently been revised to ensure its accuracy.

There have been some notorious popes and we will mention just 2 from the House of Borgia in order to illustrate this.

The Borgias who emerged from Valencia in Spain became prominent in ecclesiastical and political affairs in the 15th and 16th centuries, during which time they produced 2 popes. There were numerous unsubstantiated claims that the family was of Jewish origin.

Because of their hunger for power, they made enemies with the Medici and the Sforza amongst others. They were also patrons of the arts who contributed greatly to the Renaissance.

Pope Callixtus III (1455–58)
Alfons de Borja became the 1st Borgia pope and the 1st from Spain.
He had been a professor of law before becoming a cardinal.
On becoming pope, he ordered the retrial of Joan of Arc, in which she was vindicated.

Pope Alexander VI (1492–1503)
Rodrigo Lanzol Borgia became the 2nd Borgia pope and it was during his reign that they were suspected of many crimes including adultery, incest, simony (sale of church offices), theft, bribery and murder (especially by arsenic poisoning).
He had been appointed a cardinal by his uncle (Pope Callixtus).

During the time that he was a cardinal, he had a long illicit relationship during which he fathered 4 children. One of these was the famous Lucrezia Borgia. He also fathered other children with other women.

He promoted his family into positions of wealth including the appointment of 1 of his sons to the position of cardinal. Others were married into wealthy and powerful families in order to enrich and ennoble the Borgia family.

He proceeded to divide the extra-European world between Spain and Portugal which resulted in those 2 counties enjoying the vast wealth of South America.

He eventually died of what was believed to have been malaria.

The whole story of the Borgias is more fascinating than any story of fiction.

We will now proceed to give a brief profile of those who have served since World War 1 in 1914.

Pope Benedict XV (1914–1922)
He was credited with intervening for peace in World War 1.

He also issued the 1917 Code of Canon Law and supported the missionaries in the New World.

Pope Pius X1 (1922–1939)
He signed the Lateran Treaties with Italy's Benito Mussolini, which created the Vatican City as a sovereign state.

He inaugurated Vatican Radio.
At the end of his life, he opposed both Communism and Nazism which were new ideologies at that time. More can be learned of Pius X1 from the chapter on the wealth of the Catholic Church.

Pope Pius X11 (1939–1958)
He invoked papal infallibility and defined the dogma of the Assumption.

He also eliminated the Italian majority of cardinals and was credited by his fans with intervening for peace during World War 11.

Despite this, he was controversial for his role in the Holocaust. Although he helped many Jews, it was thought by some that he could have done much more than he did to condemn the Final Solution which befell the Jews.

His reputation was questioned by the controversial film "AMEN" which was critical of him.

Further damage was done by the 1999 book by John Cornwell, titled: HITLER'S POPE: THE SECRET HISTORY OF PIUS X11.

Cornwell was a Catholic who set out to defend Pius, but who then wrote a book that became a denunciation.

Pope John Paul 11 was keen to canonise Pius to mark the millennium but was advised to hold back on this process because of the negative publicity generated by Cornwell's book.

Pius X11, who was from the traditional wing of the Church, was said by his fans to have saved up to 860,000 Jews and was bravely prepared to tarnish his own reputation rather than criticise Hitler. He believed that his criticism would have instigated a reaction of brutal retaliation against the Jews.

Immediately after the war, he was lauded by the high-ranking politicians of Israel. This position changed, however, after the Cornwell book.

His critics criticise him for never vehemently condemning the Final Solution.

He clearly preferred the Nazis to the communists as the lesser of 2 evils, and was basically thought to be anti-Semitic.

The Vatican archives on this subject still remain closed for 75 years – presumably from the date of his death.

The Catholic Church has long been accused of institutional anti-Semitism which was originally caused by the role that the Jews played in the crucifixion of Jesus.

Pope John XX111 (1958–1963)

He opened the 2nd Vatican Council and in 1963 issued an encyclical on peace and nuclear disarmament.

Vatican 11:

- Renounced anti-Semitism.
- Embraced democracy.
- Proclaimed universal human rights.
- Largely abolished the Latin Mass.

He was definitely a reformer and was well thought of both during and since his brief reign.

He also intervened for peace in the Cuban Missile Crisis of 1962.

He was later created a Saint.

Pope Paul V1 (1963–1978)

He was the last pope to be crowned in a coronation.

He was the 1st pope to travel to the USA and Australia and indeed was the 1st pope since 1809 to have travelled outside Italy.

He closed the 2nd Vatican Council and issued an encyclical that roundly condemned artificial contraception.

Pope John Paul 1 (1978–1978)

He abolished the coronation by opting for Papal Inauguration.

He was the 1st pope to use "the First" in a papal name and the 1st one to join the names of his 2 immediate predecessors.

His reign lasted for only 33 days. He was only 65 and had not suffered any underlying health problems.

David Yallop in his book "IN GOD'S NAME", asserts that John Paul 1 was murdered in the Vatican by the Roman Curia because he was thought to be too liberal on sex and marriage, and because he was showing too much interest in the wealth and finances of The Church, as managed by Archbishop Marcinkus.

Pope John Paul 11 (1978–2005)

In 1978, Pope John Paul 11, formerly the archbishop of Krakow in what was then communist Poland, became the 1st Polish Pope and the 1st non-Italian Pope in 455 years. His 27-year pontificate was one of the longest in history.

He was seen as being profoundly conservative in his beliefs and teachings.

Mikhail Gorbachev, the president of the Soviet Union, credited the Polish Pope with hastening the fall of communist Europe.

John Paul 11 sought to evangelise an increasingly secular world.

In 1984 he instituted World Youth Day as a "worldwide encounter with the Pope" for young people, to be held every 2–3 years.

He travelled more than any other Pope by visiting 129 countries.
He also used TV and radio as a means of spreading the Church's teachings.

He also emphasised the dignity of work and the natural right of labourers to have fair wages and safe working conditions.

He canonised more saints than any of his predecessors.

He in turn was created a saint only 9 years after his death. This was the fastest sainthood ever awarded in the Catholic Church.

In 2016, it was revealed that the pope had a close and emotionally "intense" 32-year friendship with Anna Teresa Tymieniecka, a married Polish-American philosopher. According to letters from the pontiff and seen by the BBC, Anna Teresa is believed to have declared her love for him in the mid-1970s when he was a cardinal. There was no suggestion in the letters that the pope ever broke his vow of celibacy, but it appears that he did wrestle with his feelings for his friend with whom he enjoyed spiritual harmony as well as long walks and group holidays.

Pope Benedict XV1 (2005–2013)
In 2005, following the death of John Paul 11, Cardinal Joseph Ratzinger was elected as Pope Benedict. He was the oldest cardinal to be made pope for nearly 300 years. Originally from Germany where he served only briefly as a priest, he went to the Vatican as an academic and served as the head of the Congregation for the Doctrine of Faith (CDF) for 35 years, mostly under John Paul 11.

He was known for upholding traditional Christian values as a means of warding off secularisation, and for liberalising the use of Mass. He also promoted the use of Latin.

He established the Anglican Ordinariate – a vehicle to help Anglicans to defect to The Catholic Church.

In 2012, on the 50th anniversary of Vatican 11, he called a Synod of Bishops to discuss the re-evangelising of lapsed Catholics in the developed world.

Benedict resigned in 2013 due to advanced age and was the 1st Pope to do so in over 700 years.

He retained the title Pope Emeritus and continued to live within the Vatican.

Most unusually, in 2020, he expressed his view that it is a mistake to consider the acceptance of married men as priests. His interjection came as a result of the speculation that Pope Francis was considering relaxing the rules in this area because of the total lack of recruits into the priesthood in the Amazon area of South America.

Pope Francis (2013–)

Francis succeeded Benedict in 2013 and is seen as a liberal and progressive reformer. He immediately shunned some of the pomp and circumstance of his office. This was shown by the way that he travelled and dealt with everyday life.

He came from Argentina and was the 1st pope to be born outside Europe for over 1300 years.

He was also the 1st Jesuit pope.

He was warmly received by many but drew great concerns from some Catholics and political conservatives who were concerned about his possibly more liberal views on re-marriage and the role of women in the Church.

Although popular with the public, Francis is now very unpopular with the conservative wing of the Vatican, who reportedly have eagerly awaited the next papacy. His main opponent is the American Cardinal Raymond Leo Burke who had been sacked by Francis.

We are told that Burke has threatened to issue a formal declaration that Francis is a heretic on the grounds that his teachings in Amoris Laetitia contravene previous teachings. In particular, his encouragement for divorced people to receive communion.

Francis is said to be an Extrovert Catholic who responds to the changing world, whereas his predecessors are mainly seen as Introvert Catholics who feel that the world should bend to the will and the teachings of the Church.

In 2017, Francis said that the English translation of the Lord's Prayer was misleading because the line "lead us not into temptation" implies that God leads us into temptation, whereas in reality that is Satan's job. He felt that it would have more accurate meaning if it read "do not let us fall into temptation".

Francis has also made a point of condemning American and global capitalism.

In 2017, Pope Francis acknowledged that the Catholic Church was implicated in the 1994 Rwandan genocide when 800,000 people were slaughtered in 100 days. The victims were mainly Tutsis and moderate Hutus who were slaughtered by Hutu militia.

Following a meeting with Rwanda's President Paul Kagame at the Vatican, Francis stated that some Catholic priests and nuns had "succumbed to hatred and violence" during the genocide and begged God's forgiveness for the sins and failings of the Church and its members.

It was the 1st time that the Vatican had conceded that the Church as an institution bore some responsibility for the killings.

Thousands of people were slaughtered in churches where they had sought refuge from the terror.

One priest, Athanase Seromba, ordered his church to be bulldozed whilst 2,000 Tutsis sheltered inside it.

The Church also helped perpetrators of the genocide to flee to Europe to evade justice.

President Kagame described the Pope's public statement as "a great moment".

6. The 7 Sacraments

The Catholic Church teaches that it was entrusted with the 7 sacraments that were instituted by Christ.

The number and nature of the sacraments were defined by several ecumenical councils over a period of time.

They include:

- Baptism.
- Confirmation.
- The Eucharist.
- Penance.
- Anointing the sick (formally called Extreme Unction, one of the "Last Rites").
- Holy Matrimony.
- Holy Orders.

Sacraments are visible rituals that Catholics see as signs of God's presence.

The Catechism of the Catholic Church divides the sacraments into 3 groups which broadly reflect the stages of people's natural and spiritual lives which each sacrament is intended to serve:

1. The sacraments of Christian initiation.
2. The sacraments of healing.

3. The sacraments at the service of communion and the mission of the faithful.

The liturgies of the sacraments are central to the Church's mission.

There are Canon Laws which make it clear who can both give and receive the sacraments.

Catholics are normally obliged to abstain from eating for at least an hour before receiving the sacrament of the Eucharist.

The 7 sacraments are described more fully in the following chapters.

7. Baptism

As viewed by the Catholic Church, Baptism is the 1st of 3 sacraments of the initiation as a Christian.
It washes away all sins, both original and personal actual sins.

In the simplest terms, it makes a person a member of the Church.

Baptism is a gift from God that requires no merit on the part of the person who is baptised, whether it is a baby, a child or an older person.

If a new-born child is in danger of death, anyone – be it a doctor, a nurse or a parent – may baptise the child in such an emergency.

The Catholic Church recognises as valid, emergency baptisms conferred by people who are not Catholics or even Christians, provided that they follow the required baptismal formula and genuinely intend to baptise.

8. Confirmation

The Catholic Church sees the sacrament of confirmation as the completion of Christian initiation which had been started by baptism.

When adults are baptised, confirmation is normally given immediately afterwards.

In the Latin Church, confirmation is delayed for babies until they are old enough to understand, or at the bishop's discretion.

Those who receive confirmation must be in a state of grace. For those who have reached the age of reason, it means that they should 1st be cleansed spiritually by the sacrament of Penance (in other words, have been to confession).

In addition, they should not only want to receive the sacrament but they should be prepared to show in their daily lives that they are Christians.

9. The Eucharist or Mass

The Eucharist, from the Greek word "thanksgiving", is in memory of the Last Supper when Christ's breaking of the Bread embraced the notion of sacrifice.

For Catholics, the Eucharist is a most important sacrament. The ceremony in which a Catholic 1st receives the Eucharist has great personal significance and is known as 1st Communion.

The Eucharist celebration is also called Mass and Divine Liturgy. It includes prayers and scriptural readings. It also offers bread and wine, which are brought to the altar and consecrated by the priest (who is God's representative), to become the body and blood of Jesus Christ. This transformation is called transubstantiation.

The words of consecration reflect the words spoken by Jesus at the Last Supper, where Christ offered his body and blood to his Apostles on the night of his arrest and before his eventual crucifixion.

The sacrament re-enacts and re-presents the sacrifice of Jesus on the cross, and perpetuates it.

Christ's death and resurrection give grace through the sacrament that unites the faithful with Christ and with one-another.

It also remits venial sin and helps against committing mortal sin (though mortal sin itself is forgiven through the sacrament of penance/confession).

The Catholic Church practises communion with only baptised members believed to be in a state of grace and therefore permitted to receive it.

10. Sinners

The Sacrament of Penance is also called:

- Reconciliation.
- Forgiveness.
- Confession.

Its purpose is to help those who after Baptism have separated themselves from Christ by sin, and who by confession are keen to seek forgiveness.

For this to happen, the sinner will examine their conscience and with an attitude of contrition, confess all their sins to a priest – usually by use of a "confessional" located in a Catholic Church. This resembles a small cubicle.

The priest on hearing the list of sins will then usually demand the performance of part of the liturgy in the form of Hail Mary's, The Lord's Prayer and others, before offering absolution (forgiveness) of the sins. Alternatively, he may ask for any suitable act to be undertaken, such as giving money to charity or apologising to someone – often after agreeing with the penitent that this is possible.

The priest is bound by the severest penalties to maintain the "seal of confession", which means absolute secrecy and confidentiality about the sins revealed to him.

Serious sins are called mortal sins and should be confessed at least once a year and always before receiving Holy Communion.

Mortal sins are wrongful acts that condemn a person to Hell after death if they are unforgiven. Having said that, a mortal sin is not necessarily a sin that can't be repented---unlike an eternal sin.

According to Catholic teaching repentance and a firm resolution to sin no more will restore the link to God's saving grace.

A mortal sin, as opposed to the less serious venial sin, must meet all 3 of the following conditions:

- Its subject must be a grave or serious matter.
- It must be committed with full knowledge, both of the sin and of the gravity of the sin.
- It must be committed with deliberate and complete consent, enough for it to have been a personal decision to commit the sin. In other words, not being forced against one's will to sin. This would therefore exclude sex acts by a trafficked sex-worker who would be violently punished if she failed to comply with her pimp's instructions.

Catholic teaching on mortal sin was called into question after the Second Vatican Council (Vatican2). As a result, Pope John Paul 11 reaffirmed that immediately after death, the souls of those who die in a state of mortal sin will descend into hell.

God forgives those who repent sincerely but the Pope made it clear that the price to be paid for an unrepented mortal sin, cannot be compromised.

Mortal sins include the following actions:

- Abortion.
- Adultery.
- Agnosticism.
- Atheism.
- Bestiality.
- Blasphemy.
- Contraception.
- Defrauding.
- Missing Mass.
- Divorce.
- Drug use for recreation.
- Envy.
- Euthanasia.
- Extortion.
- Extreme anger.
- Fornication.
- Freemasonry.
- Hatred.
- Homosexual behaviour – but not inclination or attraction.
- Idolatry.
- Incest.
- Lying.
- Masturbation.
- Murder.
- Perjury.
- Polygamy.
- Pornography.

- Rape.
- Sacrilege.
- Simony.
- Suicide.
- Terrorism.
- Taking advantage of the poor.

Don't forget that a mortal sin is only committed if the 3 conditions mentioned earlier are relevant.

Mortal sins should not be confused with the 7 deadly sins. The latter are not necessarily mortal sins; they are sins that lead to other sins.

The confession of venial sins is also recommended but not demanded.

The ultimate sanction by the Catholic Church is to excommunicate a member of the Church.

Some acts can cause automatic excommunication by the very deed itself. These include:

- The renunciation of faith and religion, known as apostasy.
- A person who desecrates the Eucharist.
- A person who procures a completed abortion.

If a person is excommunicated, the person is forbidden from receiving any of the sacraments.

Having said all of this, a repentant excommunicated person may talk to a priest, usually in a confessional, about their excommunication, in order to arrange a remission. Remission cannot be denied to someone who has truly repented their actions and who has also made suitable reparations.

11. Death

The Catholic Church teaches that immediately after death, the soul of each person will receive a particular judgement from God, based on their sins and their relationship to Christ. This teaching also attests to another day when Christ will sit in universal judgement of all mankind. This final judgement, according to the Church's teachings, will bring an end to human history and mark the beginning of a new and better heaven and earth ruled by God in righteousness.

Depending on the judgement rendered following death, it is believed that a soul may enter one of the 3 states of the afterlife:

- Heaven, which is a state of unending union with the divine nature of God. It is eternal and blissful life.
- Purgatory, which is a temporary condition and exists for the purification of souls who, although destined for Heaven, are not fully detached from sin, and thus cannot enter Heaven immediately. In Purgatory, the soul suffers and is purged and perfected. Souls in Purgatory may be aided in reaching Heaven by prayers of the faithful on earth and by the intervention of saints.
- Final Damnation. This is for those who persist in living in a state of mortal sin and do not repent before death. It condemns them to hell and to everlasting separation from God. The Church teaches that no one is

condemned to hell without having freely decided to reject God. No one is predestined to hell because of their sinful life. Catholicism teaches that through God's mercy, a person can repent at any point before death and thus achieve salvation. It is not official Church dogma, but some Catholic theologians have speculated that the souls of unbaptised infants and of non-Christians without mortal sin, but who die in original sin, are assigned to limbo.

The Catholic Church teaches that it alone possesses the means of salvation.

It is common practice for a priest to be called to a dying person so that they can repent, confess if necessary and have the ritual of the "last rites" administered to them.

Part of this process is known as "Anointing of the Sick" which is believed to give comfort, peace and courage to the dying person.

This act is also known as "Unction" and was referred to in the past as "Extreme Unction". It is 1 of the 3 sacraments that constitute the "last rites", together with Confession and receiving Holy communion.

The Catholic Church traditionally preferred corpses to be buried in cemeteries.

In 1963 however, cremations were approved, but there was a requirement for the ashes to be buried in a consecrated area.

In other words, the ashes shouldn't be taken home or scattered in a favourite location.

12. Sex and Marriage

The Catholic Church teaches that marriage is a social and spiritual bond between a man and a woman which benefits them both. It also provides a unified and stable family environment for the procreation and rearing of children.

It follows that sex outside of marriage is a sin.

Once the marriage has been consummated, it can only be dissolved by death.

The Church teaches that marriage should only occur between consenting individuals who are baptised into the Catholic Church.

If, however, a Catholic marries a non-Catholic, they must undertake to bring up their children as Catholics, and they should continuously seek to convert their spouse into the Faith by praying for them and by bearing witness to the goodness of the Faith.

The Church does not recognise divorce as ending a valid marriage, although there are some circumstances by which an annulment may be granted. This would be made more possible if a Catholic from a broken mixed-marriage, or where the spouse who was not a baptised Catholic, wished to remarry a Catholic.

Remarriage following a divorce is not permitted unless a prior marriage was declared invalid.

During the 1960s and '70s, the author was told of many examples where priests had intimidated abused wives into silence so that a bad and abusive marriage would stay intact. In other words, they believed that any marriage was better than a broken marriage.

It is interesting to note that divorce has only recently been introduced into some staunchly Catholic countries:

- Italy 1970.
- Portugal 1975.
- Brazil 1977.
- Spain 1981.
- Ireland 1996.
- Chile 2004.
- Malta 2011.
- The Philippines are still waiting.

With regards to sex, the Church calls on all members to live chastely according to their state of life.

Chastity includes temperance, self-mastery, personal and cultural growth, and grace.

It requires refraining from:

- Lust.
- Masturbation.
- Fornication.
- Pornography.
- Prostitution.
- Rape.

Sexual activity is therefore reserved for married couples only.

Romantic couples and those engaged to be married are required to abstain in order to test mutual respect and fidelity. To do otherwise is a sin.

Artificial contraception is emphatically banned, as is the withdrawal method. The natural rhythm method and various methods of science-based natural fertility monitoring are however acceptable.

The Church teaches that sexual intercourse should only take place between a man and a woman who are married together and that it should be without the use of artificial birth control or contraception.

In his encyclical "Humanae Vitae" in 1968, Pope Paul V1 firmly rejected all contraception including the recently introduced birth control pill, though he permitted the regulation of births by means of "natural family planning".

This teaching was continued especially by John Paul 11 in his encyclical "Envangelium Vitae", where he clarified the Church's position on contraception, abortion and euthanasia, by condemning them as part of the "culture of death" and calling instead for a "culture of life".

Many Western Catholics have voiced significant disagreement with the Church's teachings on contraception.

"Catholics for Choice" stated in 1998 that 96% of US Catholic women had used contraceptives at some point in their lives.

They also stated that 72% of Catholics believe that one could be a good Catholic without obeying the Church's teachings on birth control.

There has been significant controversy both within and outside the Church regarding the use of condoms as a means of limiting new HIV/AIDS infections. This debate is inflamed by the massive worldwide health provision made by the Church to these susceptible communities. They claim that there is much evidence to show that abstinence education is more effective in preventing the spread of HIV/AIDS than condom distribution.

Incidentally, in Kansas City in 2000, it was reported that there was an Aids epidemic amongst priests.

It was also claimed that Catholic priests in America were contracting Aids at 4 times the national rate according to an explosive survey conducted by the Kansas City Star. In carrying out the survey, the newspaper received 800 replies from priests, 60% of whom said that they knew of at least 1 priest who had died from an Aids-related illness. The survey found hard evidence of at least 100 deaths since the mid-1980s and some speculate that the figure could be as high as 1,000 – out of a national priesthood of 46,000.

The Catholic Church firmly opposes in vitriol fertilisation (IVF), saying that the artificial process replaces the love between a husband and a wife.

In addition, it opposes IVF because it involves masturbation which is a mortal sin, and might also cause the disposal of embryos.

Catholics believe that an embryo is an individual innocent human being with a soul who must be treated as such. For this reason, the Church also emphatically opposes abortion.

Regarding homosexuality, the Catholic Church teaches that:

- Homosexual acts are contrary to the natural law.
- They are acts of great depravity.
- Under no circumstances can such acts be approved.
- Persons experiencing homosexual tendencies must be accorded respect and dignity.
- Homosexuals should resort to celibacy and chastity in order to satisfy Church doctrine.
- Same-sex marriage is both totally unacceptable and impossible.

There would appear to be a large number of gay priests, as is evidenced by the Aids-epidemic amongst the priesthood, and by the much-publicised sex-abuse scandals.

A chapter on sex and marriage would not be complete without a reference to the subject of abortion.

In 2015, Pope Francis decreed that parish priests may pardon Catholic women who have had abortions – but only during a special "year of mercy" which ran from 8/12/15 – 20/11/16. This policy was then enlarged to allow each bishop to grant all priests, perpetual permission to absolve the sin of abortion. This more compassionate approach recognises the many and complicated factors that may lead women into the heartbreaking decision to abort.

Abortion was traditionally considered to be a moral evil that warranted ex-communication, a penalty that could only be lifted with the approval of a bishop.

Francis's decree meant that parish priests could extend forgiveness to contrite Catholics without a bishop's oversight.

The decree didn't change Church doctrine but was seen as a further sign of Francis's compassionate approach. He felt that the Church had lost its priority of mercy in its preaching and that this needed to be restored.

In a particularly controversial case in Brazil, the Church excommunicated a 9-year-old girl who had an abortion after being sexually abused by her stepfather.

It is also a fact that women are jailed for having abortions in many Catholic South American countries.

In 2015, the Belfast High Court ruled that Northern Ireland's ban on abortion breached human rights law.

The judge said that in cases involving rape, incest and foetal abnormalities, terminations should be allowed.

At the time of the ruling, pregnancies could only be terminated in Northern Ireland if the woman's life was at risk or if there was a permanent and serious risk to her health. The penalty for having or assisting in illegal abortion could be life imprisonment.

In 2016, the United Nations human rights committee ruled that Ireland had violated a woman's human rights and subjected her to cruel, inhuman and degrading treatment.

She had been refused an abortion even though her foetus had congenital abnormalities that meant that it was sure to die in the womb or soon after birth.

She eventually travelled to England to have her pregnancy terminated.

Also in 2016, an attempt by the governing Polish Catholic conservatives to impose a total ban on abortions backfired badly.

Poland already had some of the tightest abortion laws in Europe.

The new proposal was that those who sought an abortion and the doctors who performed them, would face 5-year jail sentences.

The protests by the largely Catholic population were unprecedented as public fury was unleashed.

In 2018, Ireland's Dublin government resolved to hold an historic referendum on whether the country's 35-year-old constitutional ban on abortion should be repealed.

Although a complete ban had been lifted in 2013, abortion was still only permitted when a woman's life was in danger – but not in cases of rape, incest or foetal abnormality.

The Catholic Church vehemently retains the position that an unborn child shouldn't face the death penalty because of their father's crime.

13. Holy Orders

The sacrament of Holy Orders in the Catholic Church includes 3 orders:

- Bishops.
- Priests.
- Deacons.

The holy order is simply a group with a hierarchical structure that is set apart for ministry in the Church.

This sacrament can only be conferred on baptised men. If a woman attempts to be ordained, both she and the person who attempts to ordain her are excommunicated (thrown out of the Catholic church and denied the opportunity to receive the sacraments).

This is not intended as discrimination against women, but more of an affirmation that tradition dictates that only men can be priests.

Such titles as cardinal, monsignor, archbishop etc., are not sacramental orders. These are simply offices of the church.

Deacons
Deacons serve bishops and priests in a variety of ministerial roles.

For Catholics, it is usual in the last year of training in a seminary (a college for the qualification of priests), that a man will be ordained to a "transitional deacon". This position differentiates men who intend to become priests, from those who have entered as "permanent deacons" and who don't feel the calling to seek ordination as a priest.

Deacons of either type are given the authority to:

- Preach.
- Perform Baptisms.
- Witness marriages.
- Assist only at the Eucharist or Mass.
- Preside over funeral rites.
- Give certain blessings.

After 6 months or more as a transitional deacon, it is possible for a man to be ordained as a priest.

Priests
Priests are accountable to the bishops and their job is to work with the bishops to lead local parishes within each diocese. Parishes are responsible for the day to day celebration of the sacraments and the pastoral care of the adherents.

In 2011, there were 413,418 priests.
Priests are able to:

- Preach.
- Perform Baptisms.
- Witness marriages.
- Hear confessions.

- Give absolutions.
- Anoint the sick.
- Conduct the Eucharist or Mass.
- Administer confirmations if authorised to do so by the bishop or the Holy See.
- Be selected to be a bishop.

Bishops

Bishops are accountable to the Pope and are chosen from priests in the Catholic Church. They are able to do all that a priest does and can in addition ordain deacons, priests and bishops.

Catholic bishops are usually leaders of a territorial area which contains a collection of parishes, and is called a diocese.

In 2008, the Catholic Church had 2,795 dioceses and therefore approximately the same number of bishops.

Every bishop worldwide is appointed by the Vatican in Rome.

The senior bishop in a province is an Archbishop. This is also a Vatican appointment.

The senior Archbishop in a country is usually appointed as a Cardinal by the Pope.

Cardinals are specially selected Bishops who form part of the College of Cardinals that elects one of its members to be the Pope. It is also from the College of Cardinals that a "Senate of the Supreme Pontiff" is selected to help the Pope with the government of the Church.

Eastern Catholic Churches permit married priests but their bishops must be widowers or unmarried, or agree to abstain from sexual contact with their wives.

It is normal for Catholic bishops to administer the sacrament of confirmation but on occasions, permission can be given to a priest by either their bishop or the Holy See.

In any event, every Catholic priest has a duty to administer confirmation, even without permission, to children in danger of death.

The Catholic Church recognises the validity of Holy Orders administered by the Eastern Orthodox, Polish National, Oriental Orthodox and the Assyrian Church of the East because their bishops claim to be in a continuous line of succession dating back to the Apostles, just as Catholic bishops do.

Anglican Holy Orders however are judged by the Catholic Church to not be in this continuous succession and are therefore deemed to be absolutely null and utterly void. This position was confirmed by Cardinal Joseph Ratzinger who later became Pope Benedict XVI. As a result, all Anglican clergymen who desire to enter the Catholic Church, do so as laymen who must then put themselves forward for ordination to become priests.

Married men may be ordained as Permanent Deacons in the Catholic Church, but may not be ordained to the priesthood.

By contrast, in Eastern Catholic Churches and in the Eastern Orthodox Church, married deacons may become priests but may not become bishops. The exception to this is if they have become widowers.

In some cases, widowed permanent deacons have been ordained to the priesthood. All exceptions however require the approval of the priest's bishop and a special permission from the Pope.

There is a distinction to be drawn between chastity and celibacy.

Celibacy is the state of not being married, so a promise of celibacy is a promise not to enter marriage, but to instead dedicate one's life to the Church. In other words, to be married to God.

Celibacy is the male counterpart to female virginity, implying that the celibate was not only not married but that he had never been married.

Chastity however is a virtue expected of all Christians and is a state of sexual purity.

For a vowed celibate or for a single person, chastity means the total abstinence of sexual activity.

For the married person, chastity means the practise of sex within marriage between a man and a woman without the use of contraception.

In the Latin Church of Rome, only Catholic men may serve as deacons or priests by receiving sacramental ordination. To receive this, they must be both celibate and remain unmarried for the rest of their lives.

Although there have been frequent challenges to this policy by women who wish to be ordained, the Church has been resolute in its maintenance of the status quo and faithful to its traditional stance.

Historically, only men and boys had been allowed to serve as altar servers, but since the 1960s, girls and women have also been permitted.

In 2019, the Vatican opened the door to the possibility of married men becoming priests in remote areas of the Amazon basin. This was prompted by the drastic shortage of priests in the region.

It was suggested that candidates for the priesthood should be "elderly men, preferably indigenous, respected and accepted members of their community", with grown-up families.

As mentioned elsewhere in this book, there is deep opposition to this concept from the conservative/traditional wing of the Vatican.

In 2020, Pope Francis ultimately made the decision to ban the possibility of married priests in the Amazon basin.

Currently, the only married Roman Catholic priests are former Anglican priests who have converted.

The priesthood is clearly a calling which attracts many men who want to make the world a better place.

Like any job, the vocational Catholic priesthood also carries a price to be paid, and certain risks.

Many readers will be surprised to know that between 2012 and 2016, at least 15 Roman Catholic priests were murdered in Mexico. Presumably because they bravely stood against the wickedness and brutality of the drug cartels.

14. Saints

Canonisation is the act by which the Catholic Church declares that a person who has died is a saint.

Once declared a saint, that person is included in the canon and joins the list of recognised saints.

The act of canonisation is reserved for the Holy See and only occurs at the conclusion of a long vetting process.

It has to be established that the person had lived an exemplary life and died in a way that makes them worthy of sainthood.

Once sainthood has been bestowed, it implies that the person is then in heavenly glory and it follows that they can be mentioned officially in the liturgy of the church, most especially in the Litany of the Saints.

The difference between canonisation and beatification is that beatification is part of the process towards canonisation.

In 1985, Pope John Paul 11 set out his revised roadmap to sainthood. This retained the services of the Promoter of the Faith (aka Devil's advocate) in order to question material presented in favour of a person's canonisation.

The reforms were intended to make the process less adversarial but clarified the steps that candidates have to successfully go through on their way to being declared saints. They include the following:

● Servant of God: The process begins with a bishop who has jurisdiction, giving permission to open an investigation into the virtues of an individual. This investigation usually opens no sooner than 5 years after the death of the recommended person. This 5-year waiting period can be waived by the Pope, as was done in the cases for Mother Teresa and for Jean Paul 11 himself. There then follows the gathering of suitable evidence, a detailed biography and eyewitness accounts. This is then presented to the Roman Curia who proceed to seek further information on the life of the candidate who is now called Servant of God. At some point, permission is then granted for the body of the Servant of God to be exhumed and examined to make sure there is nothing suspicious or improper to be found. Relics are often taken at this time.

● Venerable/Heroic in Virtue: When enough positive information has been collected, the pope is free to declare that the Servant of God is Heroic in Virtue and can be given the title Venerable. A Venerable has no feast day and no churches can be built in their honour. At this point, the faithful are encouraged to pray for the proof of a miracle which is necessary before the person can be canonised.

● Blessed: Beatification is a statement by the church that the Venerable is in heaven and has come to salvation. This step depends on whether the Venerable is a "martyr" or a "confessor". In the case of a martyr, the Pope has only to make a declaration of martyrdom which proves that the venerable gave his or her life for their faith. If the venerable wasn't a martyr, they are "confessors" who have led exemplary lives. In these cases, it must be proven that a miracle has taken place as a result of his or her intercession and prayers. Today, these miracles are almost always miraculous health cures. These are said to result from prayers which are directed at the Venerable who is duly responsible for a spontaneous, instantaneous, complete and lasting cure that can't be explained by doctors. This permits the process of beatification which progresses the Venerable candidate to the new title of Blessed.

- Saint: To be canonised a saint, an additional miracle is required after beatification. Once canonised, the saint is assigned a feast day which may be celebrated anywhere within the Catholic Church. Also, parish churches may be built to honour his or her name. The Pope has it within his authority to waive the requirement of a second miracle if he and the Roman Curia agree that the virtuous blessed person has lived a life of extreme merit because of certain actions. This was the case with Pope Francis's canonisation of Pope Saint John XX111 who convoked the first portion of the Second Vatican Council before his death in 1963.

One of the most recent high-profile sainthoods was awarded to Mother Teresa of Calcutta by Pope Francis in 2016. This Albanian nun was revered by many for her work with the poor in India. Francis had cleared the way for her unusually rapid elevation – only 19 years after her death – by recognising a second miracle attributed to the nun. It was said that she made her voice heard before the powers of the world, so that they might recognise their guilt for the crimes of poverty which they themselves had created.

15. Monasteries

A monastery is a single building or a complex of buildings that includes domestic quarters and workplaces for monks or nuns who can also be referred to as monastics.

These people sometimes live in communities but sometimes live alone as hermits in very small accommodation.

The larger monasteries generally include a place reserved for prayer and this may be a chapel, a church or an oratory.

The larger ones can accommodate tens or even hundreds in a community where they often live self-sufficiently and may provide a service to the wider community. These services may include a hospice, a school or even a manufacturing facility such as a forge or a brewery.

The size and architectural grandeur of these buildings can be very impressive as well as forcefully dominant as per so many Catholic churches.

The term monastery is now generally used to describe the residence for monks whilst the term convent is used to describe a similar facility for female monastics (nuns).

Historically, a convent denoted a house of friars but these were later described as friaries.

Life inside the monasteries is governed by community rules, which will stipulate the gender of the inmates, their need to remain celibate as well as their need to own little or no personal property.
The rules will also stipulate the degree of isolation needed for meditation, contemplation and prayer. Some monastics are even isolated from each other.

Other monasteries and convents focus on interacting with local communities to provide services such as teaching, medical care or evangelism.

Catholic monastic life has adapted to modern society by offering computer services, accounting services, modern management techniques and modern hospital and educational administration.

Funding of these religious establishments can be by:

• The manufacturing and selling of goods (often agricultural products).
• Donations or alms.
• Rental from investment incomes.
• Funds from other organisations within the Catholic Church.

Although the inhabitants of monasteries and convents often do good work, there are those in secular society who feel that the inhabitants have "copped out" from the real world and have abdicated from the financial responsibilities faced by the rest of the population – notably the day-to-day graft and tensions of "making ends meet". They are total strangers to the art of financial survival.

It is also difficult for the secular onlooker to be convinced that the world is being improved by monastics who have decided to perpetually isolate themselves for the purpose of contemplation and prayer.

There are tens of different monastic orders within the Catholic Church, most of which will be unknown to most of society.
It is difficult to understand why there is such a large variety of monasteries and convents, and why these haven't been simplified and rationalised by the Roman Curia over the years of their existence.

Most but not all religious orders are unisex.

Ordained Catholics, as well as members of the Catholic laity, may enter into consecrated life on an individual basis as a hermit or as a consecrated virgin.

When doing so, they take vows confirming their desire to follow the 3 evangelical counsels of:

- Chastity
- Poverty
- Humility

Examples of institutes of consecrated life include:

- The Benedictines
- The Carmelites
- The Cistercians.
- The Dominicans
- The Franciscans

- The Missionaries of Charity
- The Legionaries of Christ
- The Sisters of Mercy

There are about 1 million people living in these institutes of consecrated life, about 75% of whom are female.

16. Missionaries to the New World

Christianity was spread by missionaries throughout the world, first from Jerusalem and then from Rome. They created an area that became known as Christendom.

One of the most active periods for spreading the word of Christianity was undertaken by the Catholic Church in the early 1500s.

It was at this time that the Spanish and the Portuguese discovered and colonised Mexico, Central America and South America.

The Spanish were dominant in most of these areas but the Portuguese colonised the enormous area which became modern day Brazil. This division was encouraged by the papacy.

Immediately after the process of colonisation, the Catholic missionaries followed with their fervent zeal to save the souls of the indigenous peoples.

Many of these Catholics from Spain believed that they would be able to spread a purer form of their religion, which they felt was currently being compromised and corrupted in Europe. The Martin Luther story, mentioned in a previous chapter, amplifies and explains these concerns.

In their honest belief that they were saving the indigenous people, the missionaries were often brutal in the way that they forced Catholicism onto them.

Those who were resistant to the new religion were brutally and mercilessly either forced into submission or put to death.

Without doubt, Catholicism triumphed in this battle of ideologies in so much as both Mexico and all the countries to the south of it, remain staunchly Catholic to this day.

17. Good Works

THE Catholic Church is the largest non-governmental provider of education and medical services in the world.

In 2010, the Catholic Church's "Pontifical Council for Pastoral Assistance to HealthCare Workers" said that the Church manages 26% of health care facilities in the world, including hospitals, clinics, orphanages, pharmacies and centres for those with leprosy.

These statistics are an incredible achievement and one for which the Catholic Church should rightfully feel incredibly proud.

Religious institutes for women have played a massive but not exclusive role in the provision of health and education services.

These female orders include:

- The Sisters of Mercy.
- Little Sisters of the Poor.
- The Missionaries of Charity.
- The Sisters of St Joseph of the Sacred Heart.
- The Sisters of the Blessed Sacrament.
- The Daughters of Charity of Saint Vincent de Paul.

The Catholic nun Mother Teresa of Calcutta in India was the founder of the Sisters of Mercy.
She was awarded the Nobel Peace Prize in 1979 for her humanitarian work amongst India's poor.

Bishop Carlos Filipe Ximenes Belo won the same award in 1996 for "work towards a just and peaceful solution to the conflict in East Timor".

The Church is also actively engaged in international aid and development through organisations such as:

- Catholic Relief Services.
- Caritas International.
- Aid to the Church in Need.
- The Jesuit Refugee Service.
- The Saint Vincent de Paul Society.

This phenomenal work by the Church brings help and a relief of suffering in the trouble spots of the world where the dispossessed are at their most vulnerable and most needy.

Catholic teaching has always emphasised the importance of the Lord's teachings on charity and how this is an essential contribution to be made by all Christians.

Pope Francis is very clear on his encouragement of charitable deeds and good works because of his deep concern for those who are in unfortunate circumstances. His leadership in this area is both very energetic and very respected.

18. Pilgrimages

Many Catholics welcome the opportunity to show their devotion to their Church by making the occasional pilgrimage. This was obviously more challenging before the days of easy tourist travel.

In days gone by, these journeys would have been made by foot or horseback, whereas now there is the option of EasyJet and Ryanair.

Holy places for pilgrimage include:

- Jerusalem generally.
- Bethlehem where Christ was born.
- The Via Dolorosa in Jerusalem which is marked by 14 stations and is the route followed by Jesus from the judgement-hall of Pilate to his crucifixion on Mount Calvary.
- The Church of the Holy Sepulchre which is located at Calvary.
- The Vatican and the Basilica of St Peter in Rome.
- Canterbury cathedral where in 1170, Archbishop Thomas a Becket was murdered on the orders of Henry 11.
- Shrines built in honour of the Virgin Mary and which include Aylesford and Walsingham in England, Knock

in Ireland, Czestochowa in Poland, Fatima in Portugal, Lourdes in France, and Guadalupe in Mexico.

- Croagh Patrick in Ireland is a place where St Patrick is honoured.

19. Important Religious Days and Celebrations

There is no shortage of religious days and celebrations in the Catholic Church. Some of the more important ones are set out below:

- Christmas day celebrates the birth of Christ.
- Epiphany. This is the feast of the 3 wise men (The Kings) who paid homage to the new-born Christ child and is celebrated on January 6th. It represents the moment that Simeon, the first to do so, recognised Jesus as the fulfilment of the promise that God made to Abraham.
- The Feast of the Presentation is held on February 2nd. It celebrates when Mary and Joseph presented baby Jesus to Simeon at the temple for circumcision as according to Jewish custom.
- Psalm Sunday marks Christ's triumphal entry into Jerusalem and begins Holy Week during which Catholics recall Christ's Last Supper, his arrest and execution. There are often processions where statues of Mary or of some of the Saints are on prominent display. The statues are usually covered up for Holy Week but are then revealed again with adornments to celebrate Easter, which is the biggest solemnity of the year in the Catholic Church.
- Good Friday marks the Crucifixion on Mount Calvary in Jerusalem.

- Easter Sunday commemorates Jesus rising from the dead although it is believed that Christ remained there after his resurrection.
- Ascension marks his ascension into heaven, about 40 days after Easter.
- Lent is the 6-week period when Catholics prepare for Easter, by making their own small sacrifices.

Moving away from the events in the life of Christ, other celebrations include:
- The feast of Corpus Christi (the body of Christ) which celebrates the Eucharist as spiritual food. The scripture readings for the Feast recall the Old Testament Covenant as expressed in the book of Exodus.
- The Feast of Saint Peter and Saint Paul on June 29th which celebrates the 2 main characters who headed the Christian Mission in its beginnings. Both were said to have been martyred in Rome during the '60s.
- The Assumption of Our Lady into Heaven on August 15th is a celebration of the Blessed Virgin Mary who is believed to be without sin, and therefore did not die, but was taken up into Heaven when her time in this world had expired.
- The feast of All Saints (All Hallows) on November 1st is when the Church celebrates all the saints. This is preceded by Hallowe'en (All Souls Day) on October 31st when the Church prays for the souls in purgatory.
- Sundays and great feast days are holy days in the Catholic Church. It is from the word holy that we get the word holiday. Sunday is the 7th day of the week and is therefore to be a day of rest for all Catholics. It refers to the 6 days that God took to create the world, as mentioned in Genesis. Incidentally, the Jewish Sabbath is on a Saturday and marks the end of the week whilst Christians have this important day at the beginning of the week. Every Sunday, Catholics celebrate the

Resurrection of Christ, so in effect it is like an Easter Sunday. It is taken as a rest day and family day because it is the day that Jesus rose. It is therefore the Lord's Day.

There are also Holy Days of Obligation which are particularly important feast days. The Church holds them in such high regard that it requires all the faithful to attend Mass on those days. This is for the good of the faithful in order to help them form their spiritual life.

They are as follows:

- December 8th – Solemnity of the Immaculate Conception of the Blessed Virgin Mary.
- December 25th (Christmas) – Solemnity of the Nativity of the Lord.
- January 1st – Solemnity of Mary, the Holy Mother of God.
- January 6th – Solemnity of the Epiphany of the Lord.
- March 19th – Solemnity of Saint Joseph, Spouse of the Blessed Virgin Mary.
- Thursday of the 6th week of Easter – Solemnity of the Ascension of the Lord.
- Thursday after Trinity Sunday – Solemnity of the Most Holy Body and Blood of Christ (Corpus Christi).
- June 29th – Solemnity of the Apostles, Saint Peter and Saint Paul.
- August 15th – Solemnity of the Assumption of the Blessed Virgin Mary.
- November 1st – solemnity of All Saints.

You will see from the above that to be a good Catholic, it's quite demanding.

20. Religious Objects

Religious objects are very popular in the Roman Catholic religion and there is a great industry in producing them for devotees of the Church. They include:

- The Bible.
- The crucifix.
- The rosary.
- Models of Jesus as a baby.
- Models of Jesus on the cross.
- Models of the Virgin Mary.
- Models of the Saints.
- Religious paintings and portraits
- Candles
- Chalices

By contrast, there is almost a total absence of such items in the Islamic faith.

21. The Christian Brothers

The Congregation of Christian Brothers, known more commonly as The Christian Brothers was founded over 200 years ago in 1802 by Edmund Ignatius Rice. Rice was later beatified.

Its headquarters are in Rome and in 2017 it had 926 members.

This story began in Ireland in about 1800, when Waterford merchant Edmund Ignatius Rice, considered travelling to Rome to join a religious institute. Instead, he decided to found a religious community dedicated to teaching disadvantaged youth.

The 1st school was opened in Waterford in 1802, using a converted stable. Demand was such that a second one was soon also opened in Waterford.

In 1808, seven men, including Rice, took religious promises. This was one of the 1st congregations of men to be founded in Ireland and one of the few founded in the Church by a layman.
Other houses were soon opened in Dungarvan and Cork and by 1907 there were 10 communities in Dublin with in excess of 6,000 pupils.

The schools included primary, secondary and technical schools, along with orphanages and a school for the deaf. There followed more establishments in several of Ireland's principal towns.

The Holy See formally established the congregation in 1820 which meant that the Christian Brothers were the 1st Irish congregation of men approved by a charter from Rome.

The Christian Brothers congregation then spread to England, Gibraltar, Australia, New Zealand, Newfoundland and India.

In 1900 came the invitation to establish a house in Rome. This was followed by New York where the objective was to help poorer high school graduates progress to a college education.

In 1955 a college was opened in Uruguay. People will remember that in 1972 their rugby team was flying home when it crashed in the Andes. Survivors were stranded in freezing conditions with no food or heat for 72 days. Amazingly, 16 of the 45 people on the aircraft survived. This was partially achieved by them eating the flesh of those who died. An amazing book was written about this extraordinary incident.

In 1967, the Christian Brothers had a membership of about 5,000 who were teaching in around 600 schools.

Sadly, times have changed adversely for the movement. In 2008, it was reported that not more than 10 Christian Brothers were teaching in Irish schools and that there would soon be none.

Changing times have prompted a considerable restructuring of the Christian Brothers movement which still has a global outreach.

The Irish Christian Brothers were strong supporters of Irish Nationalism, the Irish language revival and Irish sports.

In most of their schools in Ireland, Gaelic football and hurling were encouraged as opposed to other sports and there were even examples of boys being punished for playing soccer.

Conor Cruise O'Brian was said to have called them "the most indefatigable and explicit carriers" of the Catholic nation idea.

Disappointingly, the reputation of the organisation has been marred in recent times by widespread sex abuse scandals. During the 1990s and early 2000s, many cases were exposed of continued emotional, physical, and sexual abuse of children over many decades, by those entrusted to protect them.

Cases emerged in Ireland, Canada, the USA, Australia and the UK.

22. The Magdelene Laundries

Ireland's Magdalene laundries were quietly supported by the state and were operated by Roman Catholic orders from about 1765, for more than 200 years.

Inmates were required to work, primarily in laundries, since the facilities were self-supporting.

The inmates were regarded as "fallen women" and this initially referred to prostitutes. In their struggle to survive, they suffered not only physically but also spiritually and emotionally. They were oppressed and brutalised.

As time passed by, there became a new definition of "fallen women". Intakes evolved into taking women and girls who definitely weren't prostitutes, but who were unmarried mothers. Their challenge to Irish morality of that time was unacceptable.

Also included were those who may have been seduced or may even have only been flirtatious. Some of these women hadn't yet engaged in sexual activity. It follows that spiteful accusations could have dire consequences.

It also needs to be noted that despite the growth in Magdalene laundries, there was no decline in prostitution – rather an increase because of grinding poverty.

There was no incentive to review the state of affairs because of the profitability of the laundries that resulted from free/slave labour.
It is a fact that the State of Ireland and its government were heavily intertwined with the Catholic Church and that they were totally uncritical of this large structure of suppression.

The suffering of the unmarried mothers was increased by them being forced to give up their babies as well as their lives. The brutality continued because they weren't free to leave the laundries after they had been stripped of their babies. Women often ended up working their entire lives in a laundry. Part of the blame for this laid with their families who wouldn't come to collect them and to vouch for them. Presumably, in these circumstances, it was considered that the girl or woman had irreparably shamed the honour of her family.

In the meantime, The Church was claiming to be saving the souls of both women and children. Having said this, there was no effort made to protect, reform and rehabilitate them. There was of course no attempt to save the souls of those who seduced and made these women pregnant.

Examples of the religious institutes that ran these laundries included Sisters of Our Lady of Charity of Refuge and the Congregation of the Sisters of Mercy.

As time went by, these institutions were also used as a dumping ground for hopeless cases, orphans, abused girls and those with mental health problems. They also became increasingly violent and abusive, particularly cruel, more secretive in nature and emphatically more punitive. Inmates were required to observe strict silence for much of the day and regardless of their ages, they had to address all members of staff as "Mother".

Although these women had committed no crime and had never been put on trial, their indefinite incarceration was enforced by locked doors, iron gates and prison guards in the form of deluded sisters.

Magdalene laundries were generally accepted in Ireland until the change of sexual attitudes in the 1960s. Also, at around this time they became less profitable because of the invention of the industrial washing machine.

An estimated 30,000 women had been confined in these institutions but the exact numbers will never be known due to the Church's commitment to secrecy. There is no official history of the Magdalene laundries despite repeated requests to The Church for information.

We do know however that Ireland's last Magdalene laundry imprisoned women until as late as 1996. This in itself is an amazing fact.

In Dublin in 1993, the Sisters of Our Lady of Charity had lost money in share dealings on the stock exchange. To cover losses, they sold part of the land in their convent to a property developer.

This led to the discovery of a mass grave which contained 155 corpses which were subsequently exhumed and cremated.

This event triggered a public scandal which brought unprecedented attention to these secretive institutions.

1n 1997, the Channel 4 documentary "SEX IN A COLD CLIMATE" interviewed former inmates. They testified to the continued sexual, psychological and physical abuse which they suffered whilst being isolated from the world outside, for an indefinite period of time.

Allegations about the conditions in the laundries and the treatment of inmates prompted the award-winning 2002 film, THE MAGDALENE SISTERS which was written and directed by Peter Mullan. Although this film makes for grim viewing, survivors said that the actual conditions were far, far worse.

In 2009, there was another high impact documentary that was entitled THE FORGOTTEN MAGGIES. It was directed and produced by Steven O'Riordan. It was the only Irish-made documentary on the subject.

The showing of THE FORGOTTEN MAGGIES on Irish TV flushed out numerous inmates who wanted to band together and express their grievances. By doing so, they brought national and international attention to the subject.

The Irish government acknowledged that women in the Magdalene laundries were victims of abuse but resisted proposals for compensation.

As a result of this impasse, the case was taken to "The United Nations Committee against Torture" because of the human-rights violations.

In 2011, the United Nations urged Ireland to "investigate allegations that for decades, women and girls sent to work in Catholic laundries were tortured".

As a result, the Irish government set up a committee to establish the facts of the Irish state's involvement with Magdalene laundries.

Following the inquiry, a report was published in 2013 which confirmed that there had been significant state collusion.

Taoiseach Enda Kenny issued a formal state apology and described the laundries as the nation's shame. He also outlined part of a £50 million compensation package to be offered to victims.

A few days after the publication of the damning report, there was still denial from some within The Catholic Church and the religious orders involved. Additionally, they have refused demands from the Irish government and the United Nations to contribute to the compensation fund for surviving victims. There were thought to be about 600 of these in 2014.

In 2018, 220 survivors met in Dublin where President Michael D Higgins deeply apologised to the women and confirmed that they had been totally failed by the state.

23. Mother and Baby Homes

The Bon Secours Mother and Baby Home (also called The Home) that operated between 1925 – 1961 in the town of Tuam, County Galway in Ireland, was a maternity home for unmarried mothers and their children.

The Home was run by the Bon Secour Sisters who are a religious order of Roman Catholic nuns.

Thousands of unwed pregnant women were sent to the Home to give birth because of the social stigma and Catholic condemnation of pregnancy outside of wedlock.

They were required to stay inside the Home for 1 year, doing unpaid work for the nuns as reimbursement for some of the services rendered. They were also cruelly separated from their children who were raised by the nuns, until they could be sent for adoption – often without parental consent.

If a woman had 2 confinements, she would probably be sent to the nearby Magdalene laundry after giving birth, as a form of punishment for her immorality.

After serving their 1- year in the Home, the mothers would leave whilst their babies were typically kept there.

The children stayed in the Home until they could be adopted or fostered or until they were old enough to be sent to an industrial boarding school.

Local amateur historian Catherine Corless, later uncovered one case where a mother found work in England and paid the nuns to care for her son in the Home. The nuns dishonestly neglected to tell her that her son had been fostered and they kept each instalment that she sent them. This proved to not be an isolated incident.

Interestingly, an inspection in 1949, conducted by inspectors of Galway County Council, reported that everything in the home was in good order and they congratulated the Bon Secour sisters on the excellent condition of their institution.

In 2012, the Health Service Executive raised concerns that up to 1,000 children had been sent from the Home, for the purpose of illegal adoptions to Catholic families and the USA. This had been done without their mothers' consent.

This scandal was increased when research by local amateur self-funded historian, Catherine Corless, led her to conclude that there was an outrageously high mortality rate amongst the babies. The causes included malnutrition. Not only this but it was also found that most had been buried in an unmarked and unregistered mass grave at The Home.

Corless estimated that nearly 800 babies and children had died at The Home.

Interestingly, in 2010, a similar unmarked grave had been found at the Bethany Home in Dublin. In this case there were found to be 222 infant bodies.

The Irish government came under pressure to launch a formal investigation into Tuam and excavations began in 2016.

These excavations found human remains that were aged between 35 foetal weeks and 2–3 years. Carbon dating confirmed that the remains dated from the timeframe relevant to the operation of the home by the Bon Secours order. This contradicted the alternative theory promoted by some, that the bodies dated back to the Great Famine.

Corless's original research noted that the burial site was also the location of a septic tank. This was proved by old maps of a previous period when the site was used as a workhouse for the poor. It had been opened in the period of the Great Potato Famine.

In 2017, expert opinion confirmed that the vault was in fact a redundant sewage tank and also verified the number of corpses involved.

At around this time there had been a remembrance ceremony for those who died at the Home. It was held by survivor groups and was held outside government buildings.

The organisers sought:

- An immediate acknowledgement, apology and redress to an aging survivor community.
- That all single mothers and their children who were forcibly separated, should be included in the

Commission of Inquiry, as well as any home or institution related to these activities including all illegal activities.

• That an immediate Adoption Bill should be passed which would open all lifelong sealed adoption files.

Also, in 2017, Catherine Corless was awarded the Bar Council of Ireland's HUMAN RIGHTS AWARD, an award presented for "exceptional human service". Without this lady's perseverance, the horrors and the sufferings outlined above may never have been exposed and the truth never revealed. She shone a light on a very dark period of Irish history.

In 2018, the Irish government announced that it would order a full excavation of the mass gravesite and for DNA testing to be carried out on the remains.

There was also a suggestion that the Official Inquiry should broaden its probe beyond the original 18 institutions that were included.

It again fell to the Taoiseach, Enda Kenny, to make a profuse apology to the victims of the Home and to describe the Home as "a chamber of horrors".

Despite this apology, many were critical that the state had allowed this sordid state of affairs to exist, by turning a blind-eye to the obvious evidence.

This historical nightmare scenario had continued and flourished because of a collaboration between doctors, social workers, the religious orders and the state.

Catherine Corless was invited to attend a state reception for Pope Francis in 2018, but she declined the invitation.

She claimed that her representations to the Church, the Bon Secours sisters, the Archbishop of Tuam and to the Vatican had all fallen on deaf ears and her letters never answered.

The Pope's eventual reply was said by the Taoiseach to be more of an acknowledgement than a substantive response.

It is true that there were also Mother and Baby Homes in England that were mostly run by the Church of England. Some however, were also run by Catholics and some by the Salvation Army.

These establishments were also in existence because of the social shame of pregnancy outside of wedlock.

Having said this, there were never any revelations as damning as the ones in Tuam.

24. The Mafia

For almost 150 years, since its inception in 1860, the Sicilian Mafia has had a close relationship with the Catholic Church.

This relationship has been deeply criticised by many because of the Church's tolerance and lack of condemnation of such an evil force.

They are seen to have cohabited far too comfortably for far too long.

In the 1890s, Bernardino Verro in Corleone, formed a union to unite the peasants against the landowners and their exploitative mafia-controlled henchmen. This action obviously set him squarely against the mafia.

Verro also faced competition from the Catholic Church, which had a natural antagonism to the new creed of socialism.

It could soon be seen that the Church and the Mafia had a common ideological ground in their hatred of socialism.

Verro was inevitably violently murdered by the Mafia.

In 1943, the Allies invaded Sicily in the southeast in what was known as "Operation Husky".

It was at this time that Don Calogero Vizzini (Don Calo) was the powerful Mafia boss of Villalba in the very centre of Sicily. As mayor, he was said to have played an important collaborative role with the Allies.

It's likely that the Americans replaced fascist mayors across Sicily with more suitable alternatives, often after consultation with the Catholic Church. Two of Don Calo's brothers were priests, one of his uncles an archpriest and another was Bishop of Muro Lucano.

It's conceded that force of personality and local knowledge would have helped the selection of many Mafiosi mayors.

Despite a long period of heavy Mafia violence in Sicily, the Catholic Church still denied its very existence. Any opposition and challenge to the Mafia was restricted solely to the efforts of the left-wing newspapers. This opposition was maintained despite reporters often being beaten or murdered and their offices being the target of arson attacks.

In the early 1970s, an incident arose involving Michele Sindona.

Sindona was the most influential financial figure in Italy and was in charge of one of the biggest banks in the US.

He was also in charge of the Vatican's foreign investments and was later proved to be involved with laundering money for the Mafia, including the American Gambino Family.

In 1974, his empire collapsed amid charges of fraud.

He immediately fled to the USA and then in 1979, he commissioned a Mafioso to kill the lawyer in charge of liquidating his Italian affairs.

He then staged his own hoax kidnapping and arranged for himself to be anaesthetised and shot in the left thigh, to add credibility to his abduction.

Eventually, he gave himself up to the FBI and died in prison in 1986 after drinking coffee that had been laced with cyanide.

God's banker had proved to be unreliable.

In 1982, another disgraced banker, Roberto Calvi, was found dead, hanging under Blackfriars Bridge in London.

Calvi was head of Banco Ambrosiano which he had built into Italy's largest private bank.

It was later revealed that he had been laundering money for the Corleonesi and other Mafia families.

He also had very close ties to the Vatican Bank via Archbishop Marcinkus who also proved later to have a tarnished reputation.

In 2002, his death was re-examined and it was found that Calvi could not have committed suicide and that in fact he had been murdered.

Another of God's bankers had obviously proved to be unreliable.

It was not until 1993 that by terrorising the whole state, including mainland Italy, that the Mafia made an enemy of the Roman Catholic Church.

During this Mafia offensive, they attacked both some churches and some priests.

10 years earlier, Pope John Paul 11 had visited Sicily and had never even mentioned the Mafia, despite the exceptionally bloody Second Mafia War that was raging at that time.

These were now different times and in 1993 a group of Catholic intellectuals denounced "the scandalous links between members of the Catholic Church and the exponents of Mafia power".

Two days later, on a tour of Sicily, John Paul 11 whilst in Agrigento, launched a thundering improvised condemnation of Mafia culture, its culture of death and its profound inhumanity.

The Mafia's response was to bomb 2 churches in Rome and then to murder an anti-Mafia priest in Palermo.

There was little or no comment on the Mafia by Pope Benedict, but things changed with the arrival of Pope Francis.

In 2017, he roundly condemned the Mafia and threatened to excommunicate anyone who is part of that organisation.

It followed that when ex-Mafia boss Toto Riina recently died, he was taken back to his home in Corleone but was denied a full public Catholic burial service. A prayer was said over him in private by a priest before he was buried without pomp and circumstance.

It's interesting that when Bernardo Provenzano, the Godfather of the Corleone Mafia Family and the successor to Toto Riina, was arrested in 2005, he was hiding in a shepherd's hut which was small, messy and filled with lots of evidence of his devotion to the Catholic Church.

He was deeply religious, read his bible daily and had no problem in reconciling his religious beliefs with his criminal activities.

THE VATICAN EXPOSED: MONEY, MURDER AND THE MAFIA by Paul L Williams was published in 2003 and covers this whole subject very comprehensively.

It must always be remembered that whilst these ugly situations were occurring and the reputation of the Catholic Church was being besmirched, hundreds of thousands of decent and dedicated priests were doing their best to help, support and guide their congregations.

25. Child Abuse

THE CASE AGAINST THE POPE by Geoffrey Robertson QC was 1st published in 2010 and delivers a devastating indictment of the way the Vatican has run a secret legal system that shields paedophile priests from criminal trials around the world.

It's a fact that tens of thousands of children throughout the world have been sexually abused by priests who have mostly been secretly dealt with by an ecclesiastical law that provides no real punishment. Not only that but the guilty priests have then been trafficked to other parts of the world where they have ample opportunity to re-offend.

Robertson contends that it defies belief that as a man of peace and moral principle, such as the Pope, could turn a blind eye to an international crime involving his own organisation.

There is no doubt however that the scale of the sex abuse scandal came about because of the directives from the Vatican – specifically from the Congregation for the Doctrine of the Faith (CDF).

These directives required all sex abuse complaints to be processed in utter secrecy and withheld from local police and courts. This was so that matters could be dealt with under the Catholic Church's Canon Law that was obsolete, ineffective and non-punitive.

It is the Holy See's status as a state which enables this scenario to exist.

Cardinal Joseph Ratzinger was the head of the CDF for 24 years, from 1981 till 2005, when he was elected as Pope Benedict XV1.

The CDF is the successor to the Inquisition and is the body responsible for both maintaining standards of behaviour and for punishing errant priests.

It is difficult to imagine that Benedict was not well aware of the scandal, but in any event, as a Head of State, he became immune from international prosecution.

There was outrage when the child sex abuse scandal by priests in the USA was exposed in 2002 by THE BOSTON GLOBE.

This outrage was heightened by the fact that the abuse appeared to be endemic within the priesthood, and the fact that the Church had been so slow to react to the problem.

It was proven that the priests had found forgiveness, that victims had been silenced and that national law enforcement had been frustrated.

What was first thought to be a US problem was soon found to be a worldwide problem.

It became obvious that the reputation of the Church had taken priority over the welfare of the victims and any potential victims.

In Ireland, High Court Judge Justice Sean Ryan delivered a massive 5-volume report after a 9-year investigation.

The Ryan report revealed again that there was a policy of cover-up and protection for offending priests and that the victims included children who had learning disabilities, and those who were physically and mentally impaired. The abuse included many cases of rape.

The Ryan report was followed in 2009 by The Murphy Report that was even more devastating.

It analysed the cases of 46 paedophile priests who had between them abused thousands of children.

During this investigation, the investigating commission was repeatedly and continuously obstructed by the Vatican which refused to reply to questions. This amounted to a clear obstruction of criminal justice.

The US scandals of 2002 and the Ireland scandals of 2009 were followed in 2010 by scandals throughout Europe.

One of the worst was that of Austrian Cardinal Groer who had molested an estimated 2,000 boys during a 20-year period.

Robertson claims that both Ratzinger and John Paul 11 were complicit in his escape from criminal justice.

It has been suggested that European scandals may in time pale by comparison to the sexual abuse of children by priests in the developing world, especially in Latin America and Africa.

Incidentally, victims who were offered compensation could only receive it if they bound themselves to life-long confidentiality agreements. This process was overseen by Cardinal Ratzinger as head of the CDF (Between 1981–2005), and then as Pope.

It was analysed that the priest has God-like powers in the eyes of children, who from the age of 7, see the priest convert bread and wine into the body and blood of Christ.

The child also has to confess his sins to the priest who, God-like, dispenses forgiveness.

This combination results in a reverential fear that makes children feel that they cannot deny the priest's requests.

It was exposed that victims had been either bribed by promises of absolution or threatened by eternal damnation, if their abuse was reported.

One has to remember that Catholics are indoctrinated from childhood to believe that priests take the place of Jesus Christ, and are therefore to be obeyed at all costs and never to be questioned or criticised.

By 2010, legal claims against the Catholic Church had reached about $2 billion.

It is projected that this sum will rise to around a staggering $5 billion.

It was then found that a number of USA dioceses had declared themselves to be bankrupt in order to avoid huge compensation payments.

What moral blindness has made a church renowned for its benevolence, so reluctant to root out and punish all the child abusers within its ranks, and even willingly to move them on to greener pastures with unsuspecting flocks?

It is felt by some that the commitment to celibacy and the church's condemnation of masturbation as a mortal sin, sets up a massive tension for many priests.

Senior churchmen have accepted that up to 50% of priests are in some way "sexually active", and sadly that 5-10% are sexually active with children.

The prevalence of masturbation in seminaries and the ready forgiveness in confession is thought to form a cycle of guilt that binds clerics and confessors together. And as a result, secret sexual transgressions become minimalised and trivialised – even sex with minors becomes just another sin to be forgiven.

It's interesting to note that during the 24 years when Cardinal Ratzinger was Head of the CDF, it excommunicated several supporters of "liberation theology" and supporters of the ordination of women.

There were no recorded excommunications of paedophile priests during this time frame.

In 2019, a new edict by Pope Francis, compelled all Catholic priests and nuns to report any incidents or allegations of clerical sexual abuse at any level of the Church. This would also include any "well-founded" suspicions.

They were also demanded to report any attempts to cover up the sexual abuse of children and adults – as well as any cases of clerics found in possession of child pornography.

This edict is seen as a massive step forward in solving this historic problem.

Previously, reporting abuse had been a matter of individual conscience.

Also in 2019, Pope Francis admitted that clerics had sexually abused nuns and that in one case they were kept as sex slaves.

He reported that Pope Benedict was forced to close down an entire congregation of nuns who were being abused by priests in France.

In some cases, the nuns were forced to abort the priest's children – something that the Catholic Church clearly and without reservation, forbids.

Another severe blow to the reputation of the Catholic Church occurred in 2019, when Cardinal George Pell of Australia, was found guilty of child abuse.

Pell was number 3 in the Vatican hierarchy – he was one of Francis's top advisers and the de facto finance chief for the Vatican.

He was the highest-ranking official in the Vatican to have been found guilty of such heinous crimes and of so completely denigrating the reputation of the Catholic Church.

Pell appealed against his conviction and this appeal was dismissed.

Yet another example of the abuse of power.

In 2020, after this book had been completed, but just before it was sent to the publishers, the High Court of Australia, quashed Pell's conviction and set aside the appeal decision.

Pell remains under separate investigation by the Vatican's CDF regarding these allegations of abuse.

It's good to remember that a man is innocent until he is proven guilty.

We have recently seen umpteen examples of people in power abusing that power by sexually abusing those who look up to them or over whom they have authority.

We have seen it manifested by sports coaches, business leaders, show business moguls, as well as church officials – and this includes denominations other than the Catholic Church.

The abuse of power is the one thing which they all have in common.

We again have to remember that there are over 400,000 Catholic priests and that the vast majority of them dedicate their lives to faithfully serving their congregations and their parishes.

26. Silenced Children

The lid has been well and truly lifted off of the endemic problem of child sex abuse by priests, as shown in the previous chapter.

What has been less revealed and discussed is the amount of sexual activity by priests which led to the birth of children whose existences then needed to be airbrushed from history.

In 2019, in France, the French association of "The Children of Silence" met with bishops of the Catholic Church in order to talk about their fathers, as well as their neglect, humiliation and suffering over the years.

The existence of these children is clearly a sensitive issue for the Church, which expects priests to adhere to the strict rule of celibacy.

Sometimes these children were the result of a priest's relationship with one of their congregation and sometimes from a relationship with a nun who had also broken the vow of celibacy.

One woman related how she didn't meet her father until she was 9 years of age, at which time, he had left the priesthood.

Another recalled how she kept silent to protect her family, fearing that if the truth about her parents became known, she could have been taken into care.

Thankfully, it is now recognised by the Church that children's well-being is paramount, although it is unclear what actions will be taken against priests who have been involved in this sad chain of events.

Possibly the most high-profile case on the subject of Silenced Children, had come to public attention a few years earlier.

Bishop Eamonn Casey was both high ranking and highly profiled in the Catholic Church.

He was initially Bishop of Kerry and then Bishop of Galway. He was also an extrovert and good company. Not only this but he was respected for his work with the homeless and for his progressive views.

These qualities resulted in him being chosen to host Pope John Paul 11 when he visited Galway in 1979.

It therefore came as a shock when Casey was required to resign in 1992 after it was exposed that he had fathered a son named Peter in 1974, with the American divorcee Annie Murphy.

The exposure resulted when Annie Murphy pursued Eamonn Casey for financial assistance to pay for Peter's education. He had apparently done so with $100,000 that he had siphoned from Church funds, although it's true that he later replaced the money by a series of donations that he had collected.

Annie Murphy was persuaded to appear on the Irish TV's Late Show in 1993.

On this program she was vilified by both the host Gay Byrne and by the studio audience.

The upshot was that in 1993, Murphy became a hate figure in both Ireland and in Catholic America.

In the meantime, Casey had been ordered by Rome to be a missionary priest for 6 years in Ecuador.

He eventually returned to Galway where he died in 2017.

More was to come, however.

In 2019, Casey's niece, now 56, confirmed that he had raped her when she was 5 years old, and that he had sexually abused her for many years after that.

She described the pain and anguish as devastating.

Two other women also came forward to say that they were also sexually abused by him when they were children and that financial settlements had been made to them at the time.

The revelation of Casey as a paedophile was just another body blow to the Irish Catholic Church which was still reeling from a sea of scandals.

27. The Wealth of the Roman Catholic Church

The wealth of the Catholic Church is still cloaked in tremendous secrecy.

What we do know however, is that it was born into poverty when it arrived in Rome from Jerusalem. And that it was not only poor but also persecuted.

In 313 AD, Emperor Constantine removed any persecution of the Church and a few years later, made it the official religion of the Roman Empire.

Constantine clearly couldn't have a poverty-stricken religion as the official religion of his mighty empire, and so he re-branded it by lavishing vast wealth and huge status on the pope and his church.

With this increase in wealth and status came the increase in pomp and circumstance which is still prevalent today.

The Roman Empire eventually faded, but the Roman Catholic Church continued with its wealth and power.

In fact, it became even richer as it acquired much of Italy as Papal States which then paid taxes to the Vatican in Rome.

Also, by this time, many of Europe's countries had adopted the Catholic Church and they in turn also paid taxes to Rome.

All was proceeding swimmingly well until Garibaldi set about uniting Italy into a single nation. This he achieved in 1860, by stripping away from the Vatican all the Papal states, with the solitary exception of Rome. And even this was stripped away from the Vatican in 1870.

The net result was that the Vatican was depleted of all the taxes which it raised from the Papal States. The situation was made even worse because a number of European countries had turned their backs on the Catholic Church and adopted the Protestant religion. These defections had denied the Vatican a valuable source of income.

It follows that the financial position of the Vatican and the Catholic Church steadily worsened after 1870 until it became absolutely critical in the 1920s.

By this time, the buildings of the Vatican were deteriorating badly and were in a sad state of disrepair.

The answer to the Vatican's financial problems was to appear in 1929.

To cut a long story short, Pope Pius X1 did a deal with the new fascist dictator of Italy, Benito Mussolini.

As mentioned in an earlier chapter, this deal took the form of the Lateran Treaty.

Mussolini wasn't a devout Catholic until he saw his devotion as a useful public relations exercise.

In essence, Mussolini returned the Vatican State to the Pope and then lavished huge wealth on him as compensation for Italy keeping all the other Papal States.

At a stroke, the Vatican's financial health was swung from abject poverty to incredible wealth.

Pope Pius X1 was probably happy to make a deal with the devil because the alternative was financial extinction. He was also probably happier to see fascism in control of the country rather than atheistic communism which might decide to confiscate Church properties.

Having acquired all this new wealth, Pius X1 was keen to capitalise on it and make sure that the days of poverty never returned.

In order to achieve this, he recruited Bernardino Nogara and gave him total authority to invest the money, with wealth creation as the sole objective.

Nogara was born in Bellano near Lake Como in Italy, and although a devout Catholic, he wasn't ordained. He had however become a very successful banker.

He insisted that his investment strategies should not be debated by an oversight committee of clerics and that he should be solely responsible to the pope.

He then set about his investment plan with great vigour and made investments in a huge variety of industrial sectors.

Nogara was clearly a stranger to the concept of ethical investment because he invested heavily in the armament industry and also in the contraception industry. He also bought stakes in a number of banks – some of which were owned outright by the Vatican. He also bought vast tracts of development land around Rome at the time of the depression.

The Catholic Church had previously strictly opposed usury (charging interest), so Nogara's strategy of owning banks and charging interest on loans was strictly at odds with this tradition.

Everybody turned a blind-eye, and the Catholic Church soon became immensely wealthy. So much so, that after a period of great financial success, Nogara had to start siphoning surplus cash into secret numbered Swiss bank accounts in order to conceal the Vatican's wealth.

During the time of the Lateran Treaty, Cardinal Eugenio Pacelli was the Vatican's main representative in Germany, as well as being elevated to number 2 in the Catholic hierarchy. This coincided with the rise of Adolf Hitler who was both brought up and educated as a Catholic.

Hitler, like Mussolini, also saw the strategic value in having a good relationship with the popular Catholic Church. And the Catholic Church saw the advantage of having an alliance with the pro-Catholic Nazis rather than with the anti-religion communists who may have decided to confiscate church properties.

The outcome was that Hitler and Cardinal Pacelli forged a close working relationship which resulted in Hitler introducing a Church tax which was levied directly on all Catholics. The stunning result was that the Vatican benefited financially by about $100 million a year.

It followed that Pacelli was then reluctant to speak out against Hitler's obscene anti-Semitism in the 1930s because he didn't want to jeopardise the $100 million annual income. It must be remembered of course that there had always been a traditional Catholic enmity to the Jews.

Meanwhile, Pope Pius X1 had failing health during the late 1930s, and in fact died in 1939. According to Paul L Williams, it has been proven that a little before his death, he had prepared for publication, an encyclical that heavily condemned Hitler's brutalities. Although fully prepared, this encyclical was never published and distributed because the Pope died under mysterious circumstances. Williams asserts that foul play within the Vatican was suspected. Suspicion was increased when, in violation of sacred tradition, the body was embalmed and no port-mortem was conducted. Another concern was that the Vatican denied the existence of the "missing encyclical". The net result was that Hitler wasn't criticised by the world at large, and it is thought by some that this fact may have caused many millions of deaths that could have been prevented.

It is thought by some that from his death-bed, Pius X1 wanted to warn the world against the fascist dictatorships of both Mussolini and Hitler and that this desire could have been the cause of his death.

Pope Pius X1 was succeeded by Cardinal Eugenio Pacelli who became Pope Pius X11 in 1939, only months before the outbreak of World War 11.

One of the key vehicles for organising and distributing the vast wealth of the Catholic Church, is the Vatican Bank.

The Vatican Bank, as we currently know it, was founded in 1942 by Pope Pius X11.

His first job was to check the efficiency, effectiveness and honesty of Bernardino Nogara. The banker passed all tests with flying colours.

The Vatican Bank is not a department of the Roman Curia which acts as the civil service of the Roman Catholic Church. Nor is it a central bank for the access of others. It therefore acts as the central bank for the Vatican's finances and its worldwide works.

It has always operated secretly and is solely responsible to the all-powerful pope. It is also believed that all records are destroyed every 10 years in order to preserve the element of secrecy. As a sovereign state, the Vatican and the pope, as its leader, have always been able to act with impunity.

Paul Williams also asserts that about 30,000 Nazis were given refuge in the Vatican immediately after WW11. He further asserts that these Nazis who were escaping from the consequences of their war crimes, were helped by the Vatican on their journey to various destinations in South America. The Vatican was said to have charged heavily for these services. Payments were made in gold, art treasures, cash or a combination of all of these.

In any event, the wealth of the Catholic Church was greatly enhanced by this project which was conducted during the reign of Pius X11.

There was however, a worrying blip for the Vatican in 1945, just after the war had finished and when Italy was economically on its knees.

The devastation of war had ruined many of the companies which Nogara had invested in. Not only this but there was a huge rise in the popularity of Communism.

The fear for the Vatican was that if communism triumphed, many of the companies which it had invested in, would be nationalised. This would be in conjunction with the possible confiscation of church property.

The solution to this problem was the creation of the Christian Democrat Party.

The Vatican not only heavily funded this Party but also shouted from the pulpit that it was the duty of Catholics to give it their full support and to stay well away from communism.

The Mafia also decided that it preferred the Christian Democrats to communism.

For obvious reasons, the USA also gave financial backing to this anti-communist party.

The 1948 election was a huge victory for the Christian Democrats and it wasn't long before the Italian economy had lifted-off. As soon as this happened, Vatican investments were again greatly increased and more wealth generated.

During this period, huge investments were also made in other countries, including the USA.

Pope Pius X11 and Bernadino Nogara both died in 1958 and this marked the end of a massive wealth creation chapter.

The new pope was 78-year-old Pope John XX111 who was a total contrast to his predecessor. Amongst other things he was far more liberal and socialist in his attitudes. Because of his age, he was seen only as a caretaker pope.

Whereas Pius X11 had strenuously centralised power to the pope, John XX111 was keen to see reforms that would decentralise papal powers.

He was a progressive and his 1st job was to purge the ultra conservatives who were associated with his predecessor.

He was very keen on social reform and initiated what was known as Vatican 11.

Amongst other things, he stopped funding the Christian Democrats, and as a result, the Vatican lost control of the Italian government. This was soon to have dire financial consequences.

John XX111 died after 5 years in 1963, having nobbled the ultras and reactionaries within the Vatican. He had however stacked the College of Cardinals with progressives who were keen to share some of the pope's authority.

In 1963, Paul V1 was elected as the new pope.

He was very socialist, radical and progressive in his beliefs. Amongst other things he condemned capitalism.

It followed that the conservative wing of the Vatican was deeply concerned as to how the pope's beliefs would affect the wealth of the Church.

In truth, Paul V1 was a total contradiction.

On the one hand he was a radical, reforming socialist.

On the other hand, he resisted the reforming of the curia and any decentralisation away from the pope. As a result, the mooted concept of collegiality abruptly disappeared.

Also, his encyclical entitled Humanae Vitae in 1968 was produced without any consultation and consensus. It was rigid in its absolute condemnation of any unnatural form of birth control under any circumstances. This was an extremely conservative position.

There was a huge shock for Paul V1 in 1968 when the coalition government of Italy decided to remove the Vatican's tax-exempt status. The result of this would be financially ruinous for the Catholic Church, particularly if other countries did the same.

To overcome this problem, the pope put his total trust in Michele Sindona who was born in Sicily and who had become the highest profile banker in Italy.

Sindona's strategy was to move all Italian investments overseas into offshore tax corporations. He started to work with the Vatican Bank's Bishop Paul Marcinkus although the real authority was to rest with Sindona who had assumed a position similar to that of Nogara.

The pope's appointment of Sindona was a grave error of judgement because of Sindona's links with the Mafia. Without doubt, this association tarnished the reputation of the Church.

A brief summary of Sindona tells us that he:

- Was the most influential financial figure in Italy.
- Was in charge of one of the biggest banks in the USA.
- Was in charge of the Vatican's foreign investments.
- Was a major funder of Christian Democrat politicians.
- Was a member of the secretive masonic lodge, Propaganda Due – known as P2.
- Was heavily involved in laundering money for the Mafia.

In 1974, his enormous financial empire collapsed amid fraud charges.

Then he:

- Fled to the US.
- In 1979, commissioned a Mafioso to murder the lawyer in charge of liquidating his Italian affaires.
- Staged his own hoax kidnapping.
- Arranged for himself to be anaesthetised and shot in the left thigh in order to give credibility to his abduction.
- Eventually gave himself up to the FBI.
- Died in prison in 1986 after drinking coffee that had been laced with cyanide.

Once Sindona's reputation had been well exposed, Paul V1 had closed the Vatican doors to him, but then proceeded to make another enormous blunder by replacing him with Roberto Calvi.

A summary of Calvi tells us that he had:

- Risen rapidly in Italy's financial world and was head of Bank Ambrosiana which he built into Italy's largest private bank.
- Operated for the Vatican Bank and had close ties to Bishop Marcinkus.
- Channelled funds into the Christian Democrats.
- Eventually suffered his own financial collapse.
- Attempted to save himself by blackmailing politicians.
- Finished up dead, hanging under Blackfriars Bridge in London. It looked like suicide at the time but a much later post-mortem confirmed that he'd been murdered.

Pope Paul V1's reputation was definitely tarnished by his selection of, and his association with, both Sindona and Calvi.

His reign therefore had a destabilising effect on the finances and the wealth of the Vatican.

Pope Paul V1 died of a heart attack in 1978 and he was replaced by Pope John Paul 1.

John Paul 1 immediately started an in-depth inquiry into the problems that were causing the Vatican and the Catholic Church to lose their integrity and reputation. He was obviously well aware of the damaging rumours and he clearly wanted to make the necessary reforms as soon as possible.

His 1st targets for scrutiny were the Vatican Bank and the involvement of high-ranking Vatican officials in the masonic movement – particularly Propaganda Due (P2).

He planned a sort of cabinet reshuffle which would effectively demote those who had tarnished the reputation of the Catholic Church.

He soon found that Bishop Marcinkus was mis-using his authority in the Vatican Bank, and that he had been facilitating the corrupt and Mafia associated Sindona and Calvi.

He planned to move Marcinkus out of the Vatican so that he was far less influential.

He also found that many of the Vatican cardinals were members of masonic lodges, despite such membership being absolutely forbidden by the Catholic Church. Catholics who joined the masons faced immediate excommunication.

It will be remembered that Mussolini banned the freemasons in the 1930s as he regarded them to be a state within a state. After Mussolini however, they became legalised, providing that a list of all members was submitted to the government of the day.

One of the most influential Masons was Licio Gelli who was a very corrupt individual who later had dealings with both Sindona and Calvi.

He went on to create the powerful Propaganda Due (P2) which was a masonic lodge with a difference – the membership was kept secret.

It contained government ministers, top civil servants, secret service personnel, top armed services officers, cardinals, bishops, bankers, industrialists and media moguls.

Licio Gelli often used blackmail as his recruiting sergeant.

In essence, P2 was a fanatical insurance policy against a potential communist government.

It soon spread internationally to become active in Italy, Argentina, Venezuela, Paraguay, Bolivia, France, Portugal, Nicaragua, Switzerland and the USA.

In most instances, it was interlocked with the Mafia, the CIA and the Vatican, because of the actions of the influential and all-powerful Licio Gelli.

P2 morphed into an organisation with an insatiable greed for power, wealth and a furtherance of self.

In 1981, the Italian P2 was exposed as having about 2,000 members who were mostly Catholic.

In 1978, it came as a surprise to the world that after having served for only 33 days as pope, John Paul 1 was found dead in bed in his Vatican apartment.

Suspicion was slightly aroused because he was a man who had relatively good health and no concerning underlying health conditions.

Suspicion grew when it was learned that he had been embalmed before 1st light and before the news of his death had been announced to the world.

The embalming process obviously made it impossible to conduct an autopsy or a post mortem.

The books IN GOD'S NAME by David Yallop and THE VATICAN EXPOSED by Paul L Williams, clearly point the finger of suspicion to foul play within the Vatican.

The intended purge of the Vatican by the reforming John Paul 1, was clearly de-railed before it got started.

Pope John Paul 11 was the one who inherited this reputational mess.

We need to be reminded that the purpose of the Vatican Bank is to provide safekeeping and administration of Vatican wealth, transferred or entrusted to it, which is intended for works of religion or charity throughout the Catholic world.

The Vatican Bank doesn't use deposits to lend money and doesn't issue securities for resale or other financial products.

Its surplus is at the disposal of the Holy See, to which the Vatican Bank in 2012 made a contribution of around £50 million.

John Paul 11 was well aware that the Vatican Bank organisation needed to respond to international criticism and its tarnished reputation. He therefore eventually re-structured it. It currently consists of 5 elements:

1. A Supervisory Commission of Cardinals (the Commission) with 5 members who are appointed for renewable 5-year terms, who elect their own president.

2. A Prelate who is appointed by the Commission with the approval of the Pope. He acts as secretary of the Commission and attends meetings of the Board of Superintendence.

3. A Board of Superintendence, which is charged with defining strategy and ensuring oversight of operations. These are lay people.

4. A Directorate, which is responsible for operational activities and is accountable to the Board of Superintendence.

5. A Board of Auditors, which is charged with the internal audit of the Vatican Bank's books and reporting to the Board of Superintendence.

The wealth of the Vatican Bank has traditionally always been cloaked in secrecy. Recent years however, have seen a great improvement in its accountability. As mentioned, this was prompted by previous scandals and controversies that had embarrassed the Church. These scandals included both Nazi gold and the laundering of Mafia money.

These improvements and the current structure were eventually instigated by Pope John Paul 11 in 1990, after the removal of the very controversial Archbishop Marcinkus.

Readers will notice that his removal was a full 12 years after the deep concerns that had been clearly identified by Pope John Paul 1.

As examples of a shadowy past we have already mentioned the Michele Sindona affair in the 1970s. It was speculated to have cost the Vatican Bank anywhere between £200 million and £800 million. Due to the secrecy of the Vatican Bank, the exact figure will never be known.

Then in the 1980s there was the Roberto Calvi scandal which was speculated to have cost the Vatican Bank about £150 million. Again, the true figure will never be known. The collapse of Bank Ambrosiana and the exposure of Calvi both occurred during the reign of John Paul 11.

Both of these incidents had occurred when the American Archbishop Marcinkus was head of the Vatican Bank for some 18 years, between 1971 – 89.

It should also be noted that John Paul 11 was the one who elevated Marcinkus from bishop to archbishop.

He had considerable authority and power, which he had clearly abused during his close working relationship with Sindona and Calvi.

Over the years, many serious accusations were made against Marcinkus, including him being complicit in the mysterious and sudden death of Pope John Paul 1 in 1978.

It was these obvious abuses of power which eventually prompted his ultimate removal and the upgrading of the methods of accountability of the Vatican Bank.

There had also been accusations that the Vatican Bank had used money politically to help the Polish trade union Solidarity against the USSR as well as the Contra guerrillas in Central America.

The concept of John Paul 11 helping Solidarity has total credibility because John Paul 11 was a passionate and loyal Pole.

As an independent sovereign state, it's a fact that the Vatican Bank is protected from litigation. This means that neither the pope nor Marcinkus could be litigated against.

Pope John Paul 11 was an immensely popular figure which is why after his death in 2005, he was beatified and then canonised (made a saint) in record time.

Critics however will draw attention to his tolerance of, and complicity with, Archbishop Marcinkus. They say that it was impossible for him to have been ignorant of the money laundering activities that were so prevalent at the time.

It is also a fact that when the Italian authorities issued warrants for the arrest of Marcinkus, the pope gave him sanctuary in the Vatican until he eventually went to the USA.

Pope John Paul 11 died in 2005 and was succeeded by Pope Benedict XV1

In 2010, Italian magistrates seized 23 million euros from the Vatican Bank because it had historically violated anti-money laundering laws. The money was returned in total the next year however, because Rome's attorney general wanted to acknowledge the steps taken by the Bank to conform with international money laundering standards.

Pope Benedict XV1 retired in 2013 and was succeeded by Pope Francis.

In 2013, the Nunzio Scarano case surfaced. He was indicted for corruption and slander. Then, in 2014, he was further charged with money laundering millions of euros in "false donations" from offshore companies through the Vatican. The Vatican Bank however, was later totally exonerated.

Also, in 2013, the Vatican Bank published its 1st ever-annual report and the figures had been audited by the global accounting firm KMPG. The figures showed that in 2012, the Vatican Bank had made a net profit of 86.6 million euros and that it had transferred 54.7 Million euros to the budget of the Holy Sea to help the Pope to carry out the Church's global mission. This increased transparency was welcomed by all parties.

The general consensus is that the Vatican Bank has now reformed itself both energetically and efficiently.

It was obviously a huge additional disappointment however that the Vatican's Secretariat for the Economy was represented by Australian Cardinal George Pell, who was found guilty of sex abuse charges in 2019. He was the highest-ranking member of the Catholic Church to be found guilty of this heinous crime. In 2020 however, the High Court of Australia overturned his conviction as explained in a previous chapter.

As mentioned earlier in this chapter, it is impossible to establish the wealth of the Catholic Church in terms of its balance sheet.

We are told that it has enormous investments in stocks in every sector, such as banking, insurance, chemicals, steel, construction, real estate and gold.

We also know that unlike most stockholders, the Vatican pays no taxes on its income.

It has been suggested that the Vatican's balance sheet would be greatly helped by the ownership of:

- About 108 acres that comprise Vatican City.
- According to BUSINESS INSIDER, approximately 180 million acres of land distributed worldwide. Much of this would have been accumulated during the colonisation of South America and the dominant Catholic force that prevailed at the time.
- Priceless works of art in the Vatican.
- A huge collection of gold.

A few interesting facts came to public knowledge after the devastating fire that damaged Notre Dame in Paris in 2019.

Apparently, Notre Dame now belongs to the French state and has done so only since 1905, when all French churches were put under state control.

The French state now owns:

1. 32,000 churches.
2. 6,000 chapels.
3. 87 cathedrals.

The idea was to remove all public institutions from the influence of the Catholic Church and is the very backbone of France's modern secular state.

These confiscations were certainly a blow to the balance sheet value of the Vatican in total.

Another impact on the wealth of the Catholic Church has been caused by the compensation packages that have been paid out to those who have been sexually abused by its clergy.

As previously stated, no one can litigate against the Vatican because of its status. This means that litigation has therefore only been made against the parishes and dioceses where the abuse took place.

These litigations have put a huge financial burden on the dioceses who have in many cases needed to make property and investment disposals in order to meet their obligations. The Vatican remains immune.

It's possible that even the Vatican wouldn't be able to quantify the financial value of the Catholic Church, for the simple reason that so many valuable items in its ownership would never have been valued, because they would never be sold.

28. Opus Dei

Opus Dei (God's Work) was created in Spain by Josemaria Escriva who in 2002 was granted sainthood by Pope John Paul 11.

The movement has an ultra-conservative doctrine and soon became an international organisation.

It is also secretive; in that it publishes no financial statements and has no official membership lists.

Its headquarters are in New York and it is said to be the fastest-growing movement in the Roman Catholic Church.

In 2002, there were estimated to be about 84,000 members worldwide and of these, about 1800 were priests.

John Paul 11 allocated Opus Dei a diocese, even though it has no fixed geographic location.

The diocese is controlled by a Prelate General who accounts solely to the pope every 5 years.

There are 2 types of membership – supernumeraries and numeries.

Supernumeraries can marry and have children.

Numeries espouse chastity, poverty and obedience.

They give their income to Opus Dei and undertake to leave all their worldly possessions to the movement when they die.

They are encouraged to wear a cilis (a spiked chain around the thigh to mortify the flesh) and to whip themselves regularly with a lead-tipped 5-stranded lash, whilst praying.

They are also very strictly supervised.

Critics accuse Opus Dei of being a cult-like group because of its secretive nature and its harsh routines.

They also criticise the integrity of the investigative process by which Escriva received his sainthood.

29. Different Christian Denominations

It is accepted that the Roman Catholic Church was the 1st church of Christianity, but over the following 2000 years, there have been an enormous number of breakaway groups which have their own interpretations as to how Christ should be worshipped.

It could be said that a Christian denomination is a distinct religious body within Christianity, which is identified by specific traits such as name, organisation and doctrine.

When checking out the Wikipedia list of Christian denominations, it surprisingly presented a 62-page article. In this chapter, we will only give a brief outline of some of the more recognisable ones, but it does show how factionalised Christianity has become:

- Eastern Orthodox.
- The Latin Western Catholic Church.
- The Eastern Catholic Churches.
- Lutherans.
- Anabaptists.
- Anglicans.
- Calvinists.
- Presbyterians.
- Congregationalists.
- Baptists.

- Quakers.
- Shakers.
- Methodists.
- Plymouth Brethren.
- Pentecostalists.
- Latter Day Saints.
- Adventists.
- Evangelists.
- Internet churches.
- Unitarians.
- Christian Scientists.
- Christadelphians.

It is always fascinating to a secular person that these groups and sub-groups are so convinced that they themselves have found the answer to the worship of God, and that all others are somehow misguided.

Religion is clearly one of the most powerful manifestations of tribalism, in that during the last 2000 years, vast numbers of people have been prepared to both die for, and to kill for, their religion.

It is also claimed that in 2020, the fastest growing religion is secularism.

Numbers which support this statement are available on the website WORLDOMETER.

30. Glossary of Terms

- Apostles – the men who met Christ and who had been chosen by him to preach the gospel.

- Creed – this is a list of things to be believed; e.g. The Apostle's Creed.

- Diocese – a collection of parishes.

- Disciple – a person who is a follower.

- Encyclicals – official pronouncements from the Church that deal with universal matters of faith and morals and which are created to protect the faithful from false notions. In other words, to keep them "on message".

- Eucharist – from the Greek word for "thanksgiving" and is in memory to the Last Supper when Christ's Breaking of the Bread embraced the notion of sacrifice.

- Gospel – the early Christian word meaning "good news".

- Holy See – is the total jurisdiction of the Pope. It includes Vatican City and his universal ecclesiastical jurisdiction of the worldwide Catholic Church.

- Synod – a meeting of bishops drawn from many parts of the world, which is an advisory body for the Pope. It was introduced in 1965 by Pope Paul V1.